Managing Research
on Demand

MANAGING RESEARCH ON DEMAND

Peter W. House
Roger D. Shull

UNIVERSITY
PRESS OF
AMERICA

LANHAM • NEW YORK • LONDON

ABT
BOOKS

Copyright © 1985 by

Abt Associates, Inc.

University Press of America,® Inc.

4720 Boston Way
Lanham, MD 20706

3 Henrietta Street
London WC2E 8LU England

Library of Congress Cataloging in Publication Data

House, Peter William, 1937-
　　Managing research on demand.

　　Bibliography: p.
　　Includes index.
　　1. Research—United States—Management.　　2. Science
and state—United States.　　I. Shull, Roger Don.
II. Title.
Q180.U5H68　　1985　　　507'.2073　　　85-20483
ISBN 0-8191-5015-0 (alk. paper)
ISBN 0-8191-5016-9 (pbk. : alk. paper)

Disclaimer

Contents

Foreword

In recent decades, the Nation has vastly increased Federal regulaion of the quality of our environment. But this responsibility has required explicit limits, thresholds, and standards to implement the desired goals. Deciding on appropriate limits requires information—specific, high-quality information—as millions, nay billions, of Federal dollars flow to scientists across the nation to obtain new information on health and environmental risks. A new role has been created for the scientist: the production manager. Although members of the science community have always been advisors to the government, never has their work been in greater demand. Nor has the demand ever been so specific and so time-bound, except perhaps during World War II and the early days of space exploration. In fact, it was the experience of those periods that began the noticeable shift away from basic research to the science production line.

The transition from basic research to research-on-demand has not been smooth, however. The multiplying of government regulations, with attendant time schedules and information needs, has challenged the science community and the government bureaucrats to develop methods of meeting the demand. In spite of these information needs, the efficient production and transfer of knowledge from the research community to the regulatory policy community has usually proved to be difficult.

This inability to conduct appropriate scientific research and to transfer the resulting knowledge into the public policy and regulatory arenas effectively and efficiently is certainly not due to lack of desire or effort on the part of the Federal bureaucracy. Most large federal research and development programs have designed or adopted extensive procedures for program management based on "management by objectives." None of them, however, are thought of as eminently successful by the customers (including senior federal executives, and Congress, and public-interest groups), who presumably need the results for policy formulation.

These users of scientific information, i.e., the policy-makers, are often disappointed that more isn't available when they need it. Even more frustrated by this lack of information are the analysts and bureaucrats charged with proposing standards and conducting policy analyses. When the scientists do not come up with clear, conclusive information, friction usually occurs. Frequent occurrences of this situation force bureaucrats to become strong adversaries for organizational and operational changes. Bureaucrats span administrations and are known to have long memories. They have been among the greatest agents of change in the examples cited in the chapters ahead, especially in the Environmental Protection Agency. The dissatisfaction of delays in obtaining useful scientific information is exacerbated when the users are unfamiliar with the world of basic science.

Based on our first-hand experience, this book explores these issues from the research manager's point of view, and analyzes the social psychology involved in this type of bureaucracy. We find no fault with existing organizational structures, and find that available research program management systems can be effective if applied judiciously and sparingly. The key to improving the flow of scientific information into the policy-making arena is not the redesign or improvement of these structures and systems, but rather, the selection of the "right kind of people" to manage the research and translate the research results into useful formats. We provide a list of criteria for selecting such managers and analysts, and point out that the criteria cannot be evaluated using standard employment resumes, since they relate to fundamental capabilities, interests, perspectives, and basic skills not usually expressed in resumes.

The authors express their appreciation to Mr. Solomon Rosenzweig and Mrs. Susan M. Smith of The Aerospace Corporation and to Dr. J. Davidson Frame of the George Washington University for their assistance with the preparation and review of the manuscript. Thanks also are due Carol Bochert, who typed (and retyped) the drafts. The authors would particularly like to recognize the effort of Dr. Joseph Coleman who contributed substantially to early drafts of this manuscript. Much of the work in Chapter 3 bears his mark. The views expressed in this report are solely those of the authors, derived from stimulating discussion with colleagues in the energy and environmental communities.

CHAPTER 1

Introduction

Inventors, scientists, scholars, researchers are all professional types we associate with the loner, the eccentric genius. Stories—fact and fiction—are peppered with instances of such people who made phenomenal discoveries in science working pretty much alone, typically using their own resources. Because dreams and legends die hard, it is expected that these pioneers and their contributions will remain a part of our popular culture. It is certain, however, that the percentage of their contributions to knowledge in the fields of science will be proportionately less as time goes on.

Science is big business today. Computers, radiotelescopes, electromicroscopes, laser beams, space craft, and such are the tools used by many of our modern-day researchers. Research issues are often complex and are characteristically operated as team projects requiring numerous professionals from several fields. Further, because these projects are so expensive to launch and the people who do it so expensive to teach, there is a tendency to attempt to capture the experience of these operating research teams and to keep them together as working units for project upon project. To save the successful team often actually means the establishment of formal research institutes, sometimes tied to universities. Projects turn into programs with overhead and downtime expenses.

The only groups that can afford to fund this type of continuing research effort are foundations that are motivated toward management and longer-term results, private industry in search of advances in their product line, and the federal government, which does it for a variety of reasons. The research funded by foundations has been largely basic, or fundamental. research. As we shall discuss later, the formal management of this type of research is so loose that little administration is needed in a technical sense. The private sector research is similar. It is constrained by the company interests and the fact that results are eventually expected to "pay off." Desires to capture a bigger share of the market, cut costs, or solve emergent problems are common goals.

The research funded by the public sector is difficult to characterize. It is only since World War II that the government has put money into any kind of research in a big way. In the past couple of decades this research has generally been hardware-oriented, much of it spinoffs from defense and space programs. In the past decade or so the research activities funded by the federal government have been expanded further to include those in support of regulatory and policy needs of the public sector as it goes about its business of protecting the public welfare.

Paralleling the growth of these research expenditures has been the growth of the public sector, which has to specify the research programs, manage the funds, and evaluate the results. But experience in managing on-demand policy-oriented and regulatory-oriented research projects is very scarce. It is particularly so in the public sector. This study is an examination of how such research might be most usefully managed, how it can be transferred from the scientist to the user communities, and how it is seen as an addition to the growing field of Public Administration. It takes the reader from where established research management is today, relates various facets of recent research management experience—especially in the support of regulations—and puts forth a methodology for more efficiently and effectively managing research which is to be used in the public sector.

THE GROWTH OF REGULATIONS
IN THE SEVENTIES

In the past decade and a half the proliferation of federal authorities for environment, health, and safety regulation has been dramatic—and the use of resources to meet the demands of these regulations are, to a considerable extent. underappreciated. The annual expenditures for environment, safety. and health protection now exceed those for defense hardware and are double the federal expenditures for education, training, employment, and social services. But, perhaps more importantly, the reach of federal environmental regulatory authority is to every element of the "private" sector—not just manufacturers, but consumer goods, offices, and even burial at sea.

Between 1970 and 1979 the expenditures for major regulatory agencies quadrupled. The number of pages published annually in the *Federal Register* nearly tripled, and the number of pages in the *Code of Federal Regulations* increased by nearly two thirds. In 1980 some 40 federal agencies issued 7,900 regulations.

Direct governmental expenditures in this area remain relatively modest. But the private resources redirected by governmental regulatory action are not modest at all. For example, including interest, depreciation, operation, and maintenance, over the next decade we could spend over $500 billion complying with the federal environmental regulations in place in 1980.[1]

These so-called welfare regulations (as opposed to, say, economic ones) are established to protect the health and safety of our citizens. They are designed to correct imperfections in the marketplace and characteristically target some goal or standard or performance level that a particular segment of society must attain for the protection of our citizens at large. These levels are generally to be set by using the best available engineering and scientific information. Examples of the laws which underlie the regulations are numerous. The Clean Air Act, one of the linchpins of the Environmental Protection Agency, specifically recognizes the need for science and research in setting standards for clean air, as the following synopsis of the Act shows.

THE CLEAN AIR ACT

The Clean Air Act of 1970 is designed to protect and enhance the quality of the Nation's air resources. The Act and the implementing regulations issued by the Environmental Protection Agency (EPA) impose obligations on sources of air pollution both to achieve and maintain levels of ambient air quality and to ensure that the best technologies for the control of air pollution are developed and used. The Act has enriched our language with dozens of new terms:

- National Ambient Air Quality Standards—NAAQS

- State Implementation Plans—SIP

- New Source Performance Standards—NSPS

- National Emission Standards for Hazardous Air Pollutants—NESHAP

- Prevention of Significant Deterioration of Air Quality—PSD

- Visibility Protection

- New Source Review for Construction in Nonattainment Areas— NSR

For illustrative purposes we focus on the National Ambient Air Quality Standards in the next paragraphs.

EPA, under the authority of Section 109 of the Clean Air Act, has promulgated National Ambient Air Quality Standards for seven pollutants: total suspended particulates, sulfur dioxide, nitrogen dioxide, hydrocarbons, oxidants, carbon monoxide, and lead. These standards are designed to protect public health—primary standards—and welfare—secondary standards, and they apply nationwide. Although emission limitations for other pollutants also have been issued by the EPA, these seven "criteria pollutant" ambient air quality standards form the basis of most of the regulation of existing and new sources of pollution.

All ambient standards are required to undergo review every five years to ensure that they are based on sound scientific data and are adequate to protect public health and welfare. In addition, each Air Quality Control Region, or portion of a region, is designated as attaining, not attaining, or incapable of classification for, each standard. These designations are central to the application of requirements for the construction of new facilities based on their geographic location, and to the nature and extent of requirements on states for submitting State Implementation Plans.

To ensure that the criteria pollutants are indeed set at levels that protect human health and welfare, criteria documents are prepared which identify the health and environmental effects of these pollutants. These documents are prepared on the basis of information in the scientific literature and form the basis from which standard-setting options are generated. Both because it was recognized that science did not have enough information to be absolutely certain about the standards set, and because there was to be a review of their validity every five years, Congress directed EPA to set up a research and development organization in support of its regulatory activities. The objectives of this organization (and others like them in the government) are closely tied to the agency mission. Consequently, the time frames established by the regulatory community do not generally coincide with those of the research community, and there is a continued shifting of priorities, making research management a challenge. The challenge underscores the need for more work in this subdiscipline of public administration. This work is a step in that direction.

As we proceed to study the management of policy research, we shall make use of information found in allied areas and related issues, so as to understand their differences and similarities. Included are reviews of such topics as science and management, science and marketing, public versus private research, basic versus applied research, and federal science policy. Popular notions of dealing with publicly supported research as if it were privately sponsored and all public research as if it were (or should be) basic, for example, are much-aired topics in the field of research management. Our work suggests that they are poor paradigms for handling public policy research.

VIEWING THE PROBLEM

Efficient transfer of scientific research findings to user groups outside the science community has been a nagging challenge for years. This is especially true in the public policy arena, where decisions on major programs and policies rely on an understanding of facts and principles sought by the research community.[2] There is significant pressure when the research is being conducted for a mission-oriented federal agency, and there is still more pressure when funds are tight or the mission is being questioned more closely during shifts in the political climate. For such agencies there is constant demand for research spending to contribute as directly and quickly as possible to the solution of the problems the agency addresses, regardless of how often they shift.

Research groups, however, often feel that rushing research, or being creative on demand, is unreasonable and irresponsible. On the other hand the information that research efforts seek is often the very information needed to help ensure that the best possible decisions are made concerning a specific issue. Everybody agrees that policy-makers should have the most recent and highest quality of information available for the decisions they have to make. Forced to make decisions without credible scientific information, when such information is essential, they have to resort to political expediency, intuition, or personal counselors. Decisions are often made conditionally; in many cases a new research effort is begun or expanded in the expectation (or hope) that adverse findings will be available in time to permit mid-course corrections of the conditional policy so as to avoid significant show-stopping events.[3]

A typical example of the requirement for effective interaction between the policy and research communities was the recent thrust in national energy policy regarding development of a synthetic-fuels production capability. The energy goal of 1.5 million barrels per day of synthetic fuels (synfuels) by 1985 required the establishment of a substantial environmental research program to provide a continual stream of information to the policy level to alert them to possible future corrective decision-making, because many felt sufficient health and safety information was not available at the time the energy policy was first adopted. But enough information was available at the outset to suggest that proceeding with the program as envisioned would entail acceptable risk. If and when a national synfuels development program unfolds, the scientific research community will be relied upon to ensure that environmental data are available in a timely manner to protect workers, the public, and the environment (e.g., data on carcinogenic compounds in heavy coal distillate fractions). Their findings are expected to be interpreted by analysts, regulators, and policy-makers to make needed adjustments in the selection of synfuels technologies and widespread deployment strategies. It is this type of transfer problem that we will be looking at in this work.

Research and policy groups can and must be mutually supportive. The research group needs the policy imperative to generate an adequate level of support and funding. For its part, the research group can help reduce political pressure for premature decisions. For example, burning coal produces carbon dioxide. Some scientists believe that increased levels of carbon dioxide in the atmosphere could cause a global warming of a few degrees; this amount of warming might melt a significant portion of the polar ice caps, thereby causing widespread flooding. But no one knows for sure. The issue for the decision-maker is whether or not the Nation should reverse its policy for increased use of coal. A "yes" or a "no" response is a significant national policy decision. The current option is to continue burning fossil fuels as we always have, while the science community carries out extensive research on atmospheric carbon dioxide buildup and its concomitant effects. The expectation is that the research results will be available in plenty of time to revise the national policy regarding coal as a primary energy resource, if necessary. Science generated the policy issue and also provided the political response in the form of a call for more research.

This example of the interaction between the science and policy communities appears rational and straightforward. The frequently hoped-for intereaction is not always accomplished, however, because of a serious breakdown in transferring information from the research community to the policy community. The theoretical diagram in Figure 1 depicts the transfer processes as a stylized information chain from basic to applied research, to the policy analysis and policy assessment groups (which may be and often are one group), to the

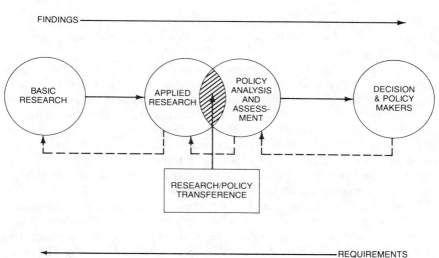

Figure 1. Research-to-policy transference chain.

policy formulation group, to the decision-makers. The latter groups can be in any field or associated with any mission or regulations. The demarcation between these groups is uncertain and often highly dependent on such factors as the type of issue, organization, and personnel involved. In theory, a two-way flow of information is essential: findings come from the research stream, are assimilated and translated into assessment results, which are then introduced into the policy stream. In the other direction, the policy stream sends signals through the assessment groups that help to frame or prioritize research requirements.[4] Such a transference chain, unfortunately, has little relationship to reality.

As shown in Figure 1, the areas of applied research and policy analysis overlap. This overlap is one we have alluded to earlier and will again as one of particular difficulty for both the research and policy analysis managers who potentially have their loyalties divided between two camps. For example, in the public sector the goals and ideals of the research community in terms of its professional standards are mixed with the day-to-day performance and reward structure of the bureaucracy. To the extent that these goals and expectations are in conflict, there will be constant misunderstanding, and pressure to yield unilaterally to one set of demands or the other. Should these managers adopt as their standard the production of research that is wholly responsive to the fluctuating needs of the mission agency, or should they support the traditional goal of the research community to expand the total knowledge base? Both goals are legitimate on their own merits.[5]

Looking at the problem one way, the science community has compelling arguments for maintaining the quality of its research, such as the historical success of its formalized system of peer review and its resistance to outside pressure to use its findings, sometimes out of context, to satisfy an exigency of the moment. Viewed another way, the policy analysis community requires research data to craft its products, which feed the decision and policy-making processes. In this vein, the policy community is obliged to be highly responsive to the fluctuating needs of the mission agency.

One solution to this communication gap is a research and policy tranference manager, to weld these two communities together.[6] Such a manager ideally would be capable of interpreting the research results of the scientist and formulating them to assist the policy and regulatory analyst in presenting the results to decision-makers and policy-makers. This unique manager would in reality not be serving two masters, but uniting both groups because of self-interest in achieving his unique objective. In the private sector whole companies are created around the very profitable notion of bringing together people who have capital to invest and people who have an idea or invention to market. These venture capital groups do quite well when the wedding is successful. In the private sector this form of information transfer is augmented by companies who support their own research groups for the explicit goal of making profits in their chosen markets. In the public sector the transfer agent can be interested in more purely technological research results than can his counterpart in the commercial sector, using information gathered from a wide spectrum within the research community to support policy formulation, or formatting research programs sponsored by a particular mission agency to support policy for that agency. This is analogous to the in-house-supported research of a private company.

In the past, public-sector transfer programs have met with only limited success. Interestingly, the science-to-policy transfer through an intermediary has elicited continuing concern, as evidenced in a recent article.[7] The fear is that the transfer agent, by sifting through the available scientific findings and packaging information for the policy analyst, may prejudge what is important in a fashion that could second-guess the policy level.

There are two polar ways of getting science to the regulatory policy community. The first is to transfer the basic science that already exists or is being done to the analysis underlying policy. The second is to order up the findings as they are needed and manage this research directly. Both solutions are in their infancy as institutional arrangements in the public sector and are the theme of this book. In the next chapter we shall turn to research management.

NOTES AND REFERENCES

1. Council on Environmental Quality, *Environmental Quality—1980*, U.S. Government Printing Office, Washington, D.C., 1981.

2. John D. Holmfeld, "Science Indicators and Other Indicators: Some User Observations," *4S*, Vol. 3, Fall 1978, pp. 36–43.

3. Blake calls this a Beta strategy. Although this strategy allows for flexibility in decision-making, it is almost certain to be more costly than one in which the best course of action is known with near certainty at the outset of a research project. Stewart P. Blake, *Managing for Responsive Research and Development*, W. H. Freeman and Company, San Francisco, California, pp. 107–116.

4. J. Davidson Frame, "Science Indicators in Science Policy Formulation: The Case of the United States," presented at the international conference "Evaluation in Science and Technology: Theory and Practice," Dubrovnik, Yugoslavia, June 30 to July 4, 1980.

5. Research managers in industry face similar dilemmas when they must balance the desire to pursue basic knowledge against the need to meet corporate objectives. See, for example, R. E. Bailey and B. T. Jensen, "Troublesome Transition from Scientist to Manager," *Personnel*, Vol. 42, September 1965, pp. 49–55.

6. Twiss identifies this individual as a "business gatekeeper," if he is functioning in the private sector. His task is to bring together the two distinct cultures of the laboratory and corporate management. Brian Twiss, *Managing Technological Innovation*, Longman Group Ltd., London, 1974, pp. 209–210.

7. J. Knott and Wildavsky, A., "If Dissemination is the Solution, What is the Problem?", *Knowledge, Creation, Diffusion, Utilization*, Vol. I, No. 4, Sage Publications, Inc., June 1980.

CHAPTER **2**
Research
Management

The research management literature characteristically addresses two general categories: basic research and applied research. Basic research is sometimes called "fundamental" or "scientific," and applied research is alternately known as "development," "assessment," "engineering research," or "technology transfer." The special field of interest here, management of research for governmental policy or regulatory decisions, lies somewhere in between these two extremes, so a review of recent literature and the external factors impacting the management tasks in these fields affords much useful information for our development of new management techniques.

Research management articles are found to be concerned with several disciplines, including "management science," "operations research," and "economics," but for our purposes the "public administration" discipline proved the most fruitful. Political science or, more precisely, "politics" has a strong influence on the public research manager; this matter is addressed in a brief section on science policy.

PUBLIC ADMINISTRATION

Public Administration has been a recognized academic discipline for decades. Present-day introductory texts provide an indication of the relevant areas in the field; the major items are treated under the five areas (with some inevitable overlap) of Organization, Decision-Making, Personnel, Budget, and Management. As in any discipline, each of these areas is a separate field of its own and, further, each has its own subareas. Generally speaking, students who read in any of these areas are expected to become familiar with the techniques available for carrying out the functions in any other.

As professionals progress and become more educated, they are exposed to the issues of why things are done in a particular fashion and are encouraged to join in the efforts to expand and improve the techniques. As education progresses further, students become less involved with generalities and more with the details of specific techniques. For example, if one were to view a continuum from the general to the specific, one might postulate, in the broad area of Decision-Making, that the next level up might be policy-making, then policy analysis, then analytic techniques, then computer models, then large-scale models, then large-scale input-output models and, finally, large-scale input-output models in social-science policy analysis—each new area being more specific and more detailed. Cascading of this type could go on indefinitely. The point is that at each terminus of a cascade (and any point in between), there is a legitimate need for study, analysis, and information.

Another such cascade, and the one of interest to us here, is found by following the Management area down a subdiscipline path which is concerned with the management of public sector resources, both manpower and money. Of specific interest are those resources which are devoted to research and development and, more to the point, the management of these resources as they are spent for science, especially applied science.

Clearly, some part of the job of a public administrator is that of management—management of people, resources, and money. Although these management tasks are interrelated, and each manager is involved with some mixture of each, we shall focus on the financial resources that are entrusted to the public manager. Specifically, we are interested in the use of these funds to sponsor research. Even more specifically, we are concerned with applied research that is used in support of public decisions. In no way is the narrowing of the scope of our interest intended to limit the utility of the work to only those managers directly concerned with policy research. The lessons learned and the procedures suggested have wide applications to other public management issues. It is simply that the area we have chosen has been difficult to deal with rigorously, has had little opportunity for practical application until recently, and has, therefore, been largely neglected as a field of study.

The importance of managing research by public sector bureaucrats has increased dramatically in recent years. As we shall see, many earlier writings in public administration have been concerned with the task of administering basic scientific and technical research. The impetus for such concern, however, has come from a feeling that technology has been a major factor affecting changes and growth in our society and that it behooved us to learn to manage better the processes by which such change occurs. This rationale is reasonable, in and of itself, given a basis for government involvement in research and development. Recent times have brought into being still another institutional change, which has made research even more important to the practice of government: the expansion of its regulatory responsibility. Many of the new regulations rely on standards of performance based on scientific and technical data. Most of the time the facts used for regulation must be developed from scratch each time a threshold is sought. It is truly fortuitous when a scientist just happens to be studying the effects of, say, a particular pollutant in a way that would be useful for a future regulation. Sometimes technological remedies may be specified instead of, or in addition to, effects thresholds. In other cases the law requires that better information and solutions be formally and deliberately sought. In all these cases the legislative requirement is pushing science. This increasing demand for scientific information heightens the need for improved methods of managing mission-oriented science in regulatory agencies.

THE INFLUENCE OF NATIONAL SCIENCE POLICY

As there are economic, foreign, and even environmental policies, so there is science policy. In essence, it specifies the role the federal government plays in the science community; it is concerned with issues of how much ought to be spent, by whom, on what, where, and how.

Matters of this sort in the areas of science have a tendency to be gigantic and, indeed, spurred on by the problems in energy, environment, and defense, have continued a five-year growth trend to expenditure levels of an impressive $67 billion in 1981. Private-sector research and development is at about the same. In addition to these direct cash outlays, some 660,000 scientists and engineers in 1980 were employed in research and development.

At least since World War II there has been a popular belief in a direct relationship between the amount spent on science and the well-being of the Nation. The amount spent and what it is spent on is implicitly translated into terms of security and national power. The ethos established decades or more ago is that such choice decisions are best left to experts, i.e., to the scientific establishment. The righteous notion that only the cognoscenti should determine the level and use of the research funds spills over into areas of professional recognition, research positions, etc. The Reagan Administration was the first serious challenge to this ethos since the nineteen-thirties. Contributing to the Administration's overall budget reduction task, federal research and development expenditures showed significant reductions in 1982 and 1983 (except for defense).

Science policy comes into play when the allocation methods of the political world are mixed with those of the science world. At such times largely informal networks and schema are used by each of these groups to make policy come into play—sometimes publicly. Both groups are very sophisticated, and both would rather minimize the potential for conflict, particularly outside their own bailiwick. There is always more demand for science resources than there are funds available, but competition has increased recently as the available funds have been reduced. When politicians become involved in the process and try to influence it by supporting their constituents who are applying for funding, or even by pushing their own pet issues, the allocation practices of politics, which are normally concerned with just the front-end of the decision process (who gets how much, etc.), are often expanded to include later parts of the process, with demands for management procedures that will ensure that the funds are spent responsibly.

Science policy also plays an increasingly important part as the significance of each of the various disciplines shifts in response to popular pressures. One year it's Space that has the headlines, and the next it's housing, or environment, or energy, and so on. Pressures generated by political desires, resource scarcity, or public interest tend to move science policy away from the autonomous control of the scientist toward other interest groups, all of whom want to share decision-making responsibility.

In reality, science has significantly less special funding status than it once had and competes with other claimants for its share of the federal budget. As its favored status erodes, the highly rational, closely held world of science policy is forced to develop strategies and tactics which resemble those of other interest groups.

MANAGEMENT OF BASIC RESEARCH

"Applied" research connotes investigations aimed at solving a specifically defined problem or answering a specific question. In contrast, basic research has no such mission, only a noble, global one: the betterment of mankind through knowledge. The basic premise is that the more knowledge we possess about ourselves and our universe, the better able are we to cope with problems that exist now or will arise in the future.

The National Science Foundation is the principal supporter of basic research in this country, and a review of its official mission statements provides a good background on the nature of basic research in this country. The following paragraphs are excerpted from the 1980–1981 *U.S. Government Manual*.[1]

> The purposes of the National Science Foundation are to increase the Nation's base of scientific knowledge and strengthen its ability to conduct scientific research; encourage research. . . .

> The National Science Foundation initiates and supports fundamental and applied research in all the scientific disciplines. . . . Most of this research is directed to the resolution of scientific questions concerning fundamental life processes, natural laws and phenomena, fundamental processes influencing the human environment and the forces impacting on people as members of society as well as on the behavior of society.

Several examples of reasons for conducting basic research were contained in a paper on the management of research and development from the Organization of Economic Co-Operation and Development:[2]

- The need to create an information base: An issue becomes visible, and it becomes apparent that there are inadequate data on which to base policy; or there is a general feeling that the Nation ought to know more about some field.

- An unusual opportunity: Geophysical or celestial occurrences that can be monitored by a network of scientists around the world spur new interest; an epidemic disease may need more research for its control.

- Research and development factors: The opportunity to match an interesting, important problem with a recognized and respected researcher.

- Pendulum swings: Heavy research expenditures in some areas often engender a need to balance by spending in others: as hard science versus soft resource issues versus human-based ones, agriculture versus energy, and so forth.

- Competitive urges: The space research program of the sixties is a good example of this; so has defense been, from time to time.

- Social relevancy: Public sentiment may suddenly demand research in a particular area, say health.

- Outside pressures: The threat of foreign competition or nuclear superiority may spur research in these areas.

- "As long as the patient is open": Research findings may uncover the need for further research, or an initial project may be so expensive that an investment in an allied area can reap considerable benefits from a small additional outlay.

- Success in a research area: Success breeds a constituency for more research in that area (e.g., space research); or progress in an area may foster the need for research on potential negative impacts (e.g., nuclear energy and radiation).

The book *Science and the Federal Patron*[3] summarized the arguments for supporting basic research slightly differently, but again we find the flavor of after-the-fact explanations of historic events. The arguments were sorted into five categories:

- The intellectual and cultural values of science

- The utility of basic research as the foundation of all technological development

- Research as an essential component of graduate education

- The high costs of scientific research, and the unlikelihood of adequate private financing

- The political values of science, especially in international affairs

Before World War II the federal government was not very active in the support of basic research, but since that time it has become the dominant funder of all forms of research. The fact that the principal patron for research has become the federal government (rather than private institutions) has resulted in several shifts in operating procedures in the science community, including how such research is explicitly defended. In the main, the principal implicit reason for funding basic research (in terms of its political defense) is the technological payoff expected from it. This changes the justification for funding from the idea that science is "good" to the pragmatic one of doing something because it pays off in useful output. This is a legitimate goal for the applied-science community and has increased its popularity and credibility (a point we will return to later).

In the meantime the shift to public funding has had ramifications for those who do the basic research. The principal performer of such research is the university. Its method of performance includes individual projects at the university itself and the development of research centers linked to the university, dedicated to special-purpose research, and staffed largely by faculty members. In fact, the link between basic science and the university community has become so close that such support has become identified with education itself, particularly advanced and postgraduate work. The universities have only recently become interested in applied research, probably owing to the recent relative scarcity of basic-research funds. But before this, the research centers, in a scramble for survival funds, had begun to investigate the field of research-on-demand. With time, the research laboratories have become more and more involved with applied research, thought to be an indirect result of the influence of widespread public sector funding.

Basic-research funding does not follow traditional federal procurement practice. Usually the government contracts for the services it wishes to purchase through open public bids, and an award is made to the lowest qualified bid. But basic research, by definition, cannot be defined precisely enough to allow the use of standard contracts. Because of this, the concept of a contract deliverable had to be modified. The evolution of this new instrument for funding basic research led to a device known as a grant. Patterned after the private foundation grant, this contractual device allowed the government very broad discretion as to the method and product of the research purchased. The switch to grants also meant a shift in the type of inhouse staff. The government, through in-house research staffs or program managers, maintains enough expertise to ensure that the funds are responsibly managed and that some measure of accountability is forthcoming. The grant, then, supports research that the research community wants to do, while the contract purchases research that the government wants to have done. This distinction is an extremely important one for the dichotomy of basic and applied research, discussed later in this section. The contract is the proper instrument to be used when funding applied research and the one assumed later in our discussions. It is, however, a *fundamentally* different funding mechanism, both legally and conceptually, than that used for basic research. This fact is often the cause of noticeable friction when the public sector tries to contract with the universities for applied research, because those institutions are more familiar with grants.

Several federal agencies maintain basic-research programs, including the National Science Foundation, the Department of Energy, the Office of Naval Research, and the National Institutes of Health.

A recent study by Wert et al.[4] looked at these agencies in terms of their management systems. We have summarized some of their case studies here.

The stages of management reviewed in the study were (1) program planning, (2) program management, and (3) program review. The three agencies investigated have developed systems which are fundamentally similar:

- All of their methods of managing research were based on the methods of organizations that were structured by scientific discipline.

- To some extent all depend upon the use of unsolicited proposals. The program managers in each of these areas have varying degrees of influence on the subject area of the proposals. Some of this influence can be direct, some indirect. For example, they develop a program plan and use various methods to encourage scientists to submit proposals. To a greater or lesser extent, the scientific community is also a stimulus to these proposals.

- Project selection is formalized and routinized, though it may differ in the details of how it is done. Although the program director usually has the final say on what projects are funded, considerable advice is sought from peers through the use of formal panels or other methods, including mail solicitations. In addition to the merits of the proposal, consideration is given to the institution and the principal investigator.

- Once a grant is awarded, there is very little monitoring of the actual research.

- The evaluation of the final product is not normally done at all by the granting agency. The project quality and utility is demonstrated by publication in peer-refereed literature. The program of which the project is a part is subject to varying kinds of review, though, ranging from those done by external experts to those done by the agency itself.

Although specific differences can be noted, in general the project grant system used by the studied agencies is as described above. The Wert study summarizes this system:[5]

> Support is awarded to a university or other institution for a particular project to be performed by a designated investigator (or investigators) for a limited period of time (usually less than five years). Project ideas are generated by researchers in the

performer community and submitted to the agency as unsolicited proposals.

The management procedures for project selection are more structural and formalized than any other stage of the management process.

The agencies rely heavily on technical advisors in the scientific community (rather than on internal staff or R&D users) when determining which proposed projects to fund.

During the course of a project, investigators are relatively free to alter their plans of work, provided that the general topic of research remains the same.

Near the end of a project, most investigators submit a proposal to continue their work. The reviews of these proposals, in which an investigator's past record of accomplishment is carefully examined, constitute an extensive post evaluation of work accomplished.

The process described here is noticeably lacking in public accountability, especially regarding restrictions on the principal investigator. This freedom, held to be so important to creativity and so important to basic research, is often disastrous when allowed in applied research. And yet, as we shall see, because many of the institutions which conduct policy research (such as universities) expect the rules of government funding to be the same there as in basic research, there is often considerable friction generated during the time of project preparation around the topic of scientific freedom. This problem is even further exacerbated when the people who manage the research for the government are also members of the science community. Their expectations of how to manage a contract, for similar reasons, also may not mesh with the needs or expectations of the agency they work for.

In general, it is obvious that the loose management style allowed in giving grants for basic research is not appropriate to most research and development in a mission-oriented agency. Consequently, for this and the other reasons noted above, the research management model specified by the basic-science community is not appropriate for applied science.

There is always a tension between the scientist who wants absolute freedom in his work and no strings on his money and the public-sector program manager who must live in the world of voter accountability. Budget constraints, political considerations, and numerous other factors have to be balanced before public funds are released. The criteria are different in the basic-research area from those used in allocating funds across several competing research areas. Fudamental-research funding is based on scientific merit as judged by peers, whereas the interdisciplinary allocations are based on political perceptions of the relative social importance of each field. The basic-research allocation process is like the one used for the military or national security; in which the experts, not the public, make the policy calls on funding. This process is often challenged in a society such as ours, where there is a requirement that taxpayer money be accounted for in a responsible fashion.

The two factors most necessary in allocating funds for basic-research projects intended primarily for the science community, not the public at large, are a good technical manager and the peer review. With both there is a dependence on expertise and high-level technical competence—in other words, professionals minding the store for other professionals. It would only be by sheerest accident that factors other than those specified by the scientists reviewing and using the research would be explicitly considered. Social priorities, such as increasing minority and handicapped opportunities in the sciences, for instance, are likely to be irrelevant to such a group in a discussion of what the next stages are, say, in astrophysics. Again, because of the involvement of the public sector in funding science, there has been a normative judgment that equal opportunity and affirmative action rules should apply to all federal programs, including basic research. Forcing such requirements into the basic research management process is logically impossible, but often politically mandatory. To minimize negative impacts on basic research in the short term, most federal agencies have employed such social program goals as secondary program criteria, or have created supplementary programs whose primary goal is minority assistance and secondary goal is basic research.

Further, the science community, because it is basically carrying out research for its own use, has not felt a burning need to justify the final product to anybody else. In most cases there is not any necessity for its members to even ensure that there will be a final product at all from any specific project. The latter feature of the ethos of science causes difficulty for public sector managers who fund the research. On the one hand, because these managers tend to come from the professional science community, they are reluctant to interfere in the traditional science process; on the other, although public-sector-sponsored research is traditionally riskier than the private, there is still a proclivity to appear fiscally responsible and practical to the Congress and Administration.

Much of the basic research in mission-oriented agencies tends to be done in in-house research laboratories like the former Atomic Energy Commission or the Environmental Protection Agency. These government scientists, although still regarded by their peers as equals, are under great pressure to stick to specific areas of research and to projects expected to pay off. To this end, one report, "The Role of Management in Science,"[6] conceptualizes science and research as a system of production. The article suggests that, when looked at systematically, science does lend itself to standard management practices. All that must be done, it is claimed, is to understand exactly the objective. The process, from problem definition to research results, is segmented in six steps: (1) ideation, (2) planning and design, (3) financing and staffing, (4) organizing, (5) producing, and (6) output. Each of these stages has its own discrete managerial tasks. Straightforward administrative questions are asked at each stage, to lead the reader to standard management paradigms for response. For example, in the producing stage the questions include: How is the work done? How is it supervised? What is the nature of the work environment? Standard questions, familiar to any line supervisor. Slowly a composite picture emerges, of a logically, routinely organized process for producing research output, much like the one producing automobiles. Given this paradigm, the research manager needs essentially the same skills as any other production manager—though the purist would question whether this is truly basic research.

In the main, there is little wrong with this picture of research management and, indeed, it is probably a fairly accurate description of how research is actually carried out in many of today's organizations, public and private. Such a conceptualization fits well those problems where the research is meant to produce a desired output that is reasonably understood by the scientist and the funder. But research that does not have a clearly defined end, or is in search of fundamental scientific principles, cannot be so readily structured. The decision rules for funding such research are more in the nature of supporting "worthwhile" ideas, done by "responsible" scientists, who have given previous evidence of being able to add to our storehouse of scientific knowledge. Research in support of public policy (i.e., applied research), the subject of interest here, is more likely able to be carried out in the method suggested above, because it is more concerned with producing a product. The emphasis of this work is to investigate why such a seemingly straightforward approach to research management and production has not come to pass in the public sector and, understanding this, to suggest how science management for policy can be made more responsive.

TECHNOLOGY TRANSFER

Another field of activity closely allied to the mission of making scientific information available to the regulatory and policy stream is commonly titled "technology transfer." This discipline is concerned with transferring the results of applied research and development to its user communities, which may be industry, private consultants, or state and local governments.

A significant portion of the applied-science research and development budgets is spent on hardware projects (new engine designs, pollution control equipment, and the like), and the question often posed is whether these projects ever benefit the private sector. Because the research often does not have noticeable payoff, there is much discussion of how to transfer its results from the public to the private sector.[7] One of the most often cited solutions is to make the public sector act like the private.

Practically every agency in the federal government engages in one form or another of research or development or demonstration of hardware, ideas, techniques, and the like. Although we are principally interested in moving nonhardware research results from the research community to the public policy arena, many insights can be gained by looking first at the difficulty of transferring research on technologies into the marketplace, for clues to why there is also difficulty with moving research ideas into policy areas.

Problems

One way to analyze the low rate of adoption and diffusion of technologies developed with public funds is to compare the research and development processes in the private and public sectors. In reviewing these in terms of their differences in orientation, setting, and behavior, four generic areas have been identified, in which conditions and extraneous influences interact with the research and development in such a way as to frustrate the commercialization of government-sponsored R&D: (1) role and motivation, (2) project selection and termination criteria, (3) client relationships, and (4) conduct of the work.

Of these the most fundamental difference between the public and private activities is found in the first—role and motivation of the people engaged in the work. Private R&D is a business activity that pursues profit-making opportunities by responding to, or in some cases creating, market demands.[8] In contrast, most government-sponsored R&D is agency-responsive.[9] Whereas private companies are market-focused, governmental agencies tend to be mission-oriented and dedicated to addressing specific societal concerns: housing, transportation, environment, etc.

Agency-responsiveness and mission orientation lead government agencies to organize technology R&D programs around "the proof of concepts." The often-perceived objective is to establish the feasibility of a technology that advances the state of the art within a specific mission area, such as pollution control (e.g., scrubbers, catalytic converters), energy conservation (e.g., fluidized-bed combustion, pyrolysis cookers), transportation (e.g., the electric car), and even manned space flight. Once the feasibility of the technology is demonstrated and documented, the research and development are considered complete, and the project is terminated.

In contrast, the private sector's R&D programs have a success standard based on "the proof of sales."[10] The perceived ultimate objective is to develop a product that can be marketed profitably. Marketability requires that the technology perform in multiple dimensions—dimensions broader than the mandate of a mission-oriented agency. Thus, the marketability criterion imposes, simultaneously, tests of performance, price competitiveness, consumer acceptance, and manufacturability.[11] It would only be by chance that the success standards of these two sectors were the same for any particular product.

These differences in project and product criteria are exaggerated by differences in the client relationships between government agencies and the private sector entities. Businesses tend to shape their R&D programs around service markets where they have already established reputations, expertise, and sales networks. By "leading from strength" businesses avoid or reduce the risks and uncertainties that are associated with new clients, new markets, and new products. The production and sales activities of the firm can be scheduled and made efficiently routine because the consumer or client has relatively well-known and predictable wants and needs. Research and development focused on incremental improvements in product design supports this continuity of clientele and marketing strategy.[12]

Public sector agencies must typically serve and satisfy a more diverse clientele, and this places conflicting demands on their staff and budget. Federal agencies must frequently position themselves to satisfy simultaneously congressional policy (with appropriations and authorizing committees frequently at loggerheads), Office of Management and Budget examiners, cabinet-level coordinating committees (such as the old Domestic Council or the new Cabinet Councils), industrial clients, and implementing agencies at the state and local levels. Budget competition and "turf" conflicts between agencies further complicate the definitions of government R&D objectives.[13]

The cross-pressures of conflicting demands influence the mix of R&D projects and can distort the outcome of particular activities. Critical to the issue of implementation failure is the fact that "signals" from potential users or manufacturers of a technology are muted by demands from the political process and the exigencies of agency politics. The demands of competing constituencies are amplified by the fragmentation of authority in the public sector.

There is a substantial exchange of personnel among government, private industry, consulting firms, and universities. This tends to dilute their differences. Although the R&D techniques are similar in the two sectors, differences abound. Probably the most critical one is between the multidisciplinary activities in the private sector and the stronger disciplinary biases in the public agencies.

Federal R&D activities display what might be considered a significant engineering bias, while private sector R&D is shaped by orchestrated interaction between design technicians, marketing specialists, financial analysts, cost-control engineers, and practitioners from sales and production. The engineering optima and cost-conscious design are substantially different. Public implementing agencies— typically state or local agencies—display biases comparable to those of federal agencies. Local agencies tend toward capital-intensive, engineered, or "built" solutions that can be programmed as projects. Routinization and a limited array of solution strategies—a limited product line—is a trademark of local implementing agencies, as it is of the federal agencies.

A final, and perhaps the most basic, difference between the private and public sectors in conducting research and development is the extent to which implementation and marketability concerns are integral components of the two sectors' processes. In the private sector, marketing management plays a major role in decision-making throughout all stages of the R&D process.[14] In the public sector, however, implementation and marketing are generally not considered at all or not until the final stages.

The process operating in both sectors is presented schematically in Figure 2, which illustrates some of the principal differences in orientation and priority. Project origin, project organization and evaluation, and implementation and end-user orientation are among the differences characterized. This figure also distinguishes between a "minimal survival path," which is followed by the federal agency, and the "full implementation path," which is essentially within the domain of the private sector or local implementation agency, directly orienting products and services to the end user.

The differences in role, behavior, motivation, and clientele described above are clues to why the products of federally sponsored R&D fail to achieve greater acceptance in the commercial marketplace and the area of state and local government. The failure may be a function of market incompatibility: the dissonance between a candidate technology and the wants and requisites of the manufac-

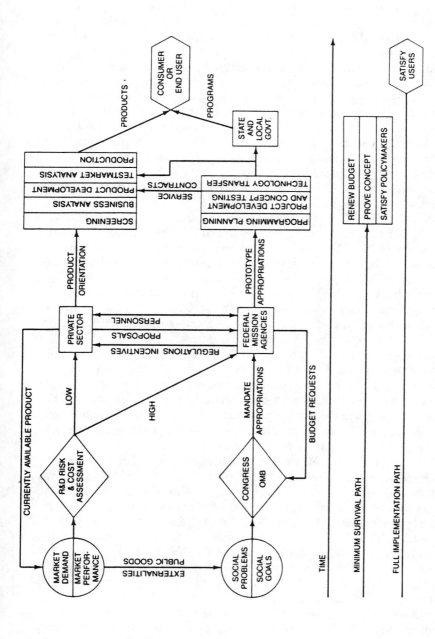

Figure 2. Research and development (R&D) process in the public and private sectors. OMB, Office of Management and Budget.

turers and consumers. That is, implementation failure would occur because the technology was out of synchronization with consumer desires or with the structure of incentives guiding the policy decisions of the firms making up the technology delivery system.[15] Or implementation failure may be a function of market failure—the dissonance between private wants and social needs. In the latter case failure might occur because the technology delivery system was not motivated to achieve policy-defined notions of social welfare but to serve the private interests of producers and those consumers whose incomes were sufficient in the aggregate to constitute a market.

Marketing and market research tend to be an afterthought in the public sector. Marketing techniques are often used in disseminating research findings and information about prototypes, but they tend to play only a limited role in shaping the R&D agenda and the process of technology design.

Public sector R&D managers feel pressure to stay off the private sector's turf and to avoid downstream activities preempted by profit-seeking capital.[16] The sometimes adversary, sometimes collaborative, relationship between mission-oriented agencies and private firms serves to confine the government efforts to high-risk, complex system research having a high probability of implementation failure. It is such high-risk, long-term programs that are seen by many as proper areas for research, and so the technology transfer is often frustrated by trying to follow two often opposed paths.

Policy-making and public expenditures typically take place in a bureaucratic setting of Byzantine complexity. Agency outputs must satisfy a large number of constituencies, only two of which are composed of producers and end-point consumers. To the extent that agency outputs are shaped by political or institutional demands, they may be unsuited to satisfying the requirements of manufacturability, profitability, and consumer acceptance.

Most agencies do not have explicit objectives or rules for making tradeoffs between objectives. "Best judgment" and "rules of thumb" tend to prevail. This is a consequence, in part, of the multiple demands placed on them and, in part, of a modus operandi that emphasizes the pursuit of relatively narrow, mission-oriented goals.

Competition is ritually favored in the private sector, where it is associated with product and price differentiation and economic efficiency. In the public sector it tends to be expressed in terms of rivalries over turfs and domains, coupled with suspicions of inefficient and unnecessary duplication of effort.

Failure to implement, or less than effectively implement, may be a consequence of the same economic forces that require public intervention. When public intervention is precipitated by externalities, income inequalities, the aversion of oligopolistic capital to risk, or other forms of market failure, it is reasonable to look for the causes in the structure of the economy rather than in the shortcomings of a particular research and development agency.

Federal R&D has historically and traditionally been conducted to serve recognized public needs: the military, public health, agriculture, the space program, and implementation agencies at the state and local level. Commercial and industrial firms are a relatively new, but normally secondary, client group for federally sponsored R&D. It appears that the screening criteria have not been modified to incorporate the requirements of private implementation.

In a work entitled *Getting It Off the Shelf*, eleven case studies were conducted, three focusing on a technology program designed for a local government client, two on projects in a social welfare context, two on projects with a private sector client, and four on projects with a private client motivated by regulations and subsidies.[17] No studies were undertaken in the case of the military and space programs, which account for the majority of federal R&D activity, because the authors recognized the special problems in procurement there, involving issues fundamentally different from those of technology adoption in civilian markets. The following table[18] shows the case selection and summary description of the cases studied.

Market	*Cases*
State or local government infrastructure programs (public goods)	Urban information systems
	Transportation system management
	Personal rapid transit
Social welfare programs motivated by minimum standards of well-being (merit goods)	Housing rehabilitation ("instant rehab")
	New towns
The military and space program	None
The private sector motivated by the traditional incentive of return on investment	Commuter aircraft
	Poultry waste process
The private sector motivated by governmental incentives, penalties, or regulations	Jet engine retrofit and noise suppression
	Stack gas desulfurization
	Seat belts and airbags
	Transbus

The case studies tested the general hypothesis that the failure of technology adoption and diffusion is most likely to occur where the "push of policy and the pull of markets" are dissonant or mismatched. To explore the merit of this hypothesis, they focused on four questions concerning R&D planning and execution:

- Was market demand considered in the screening and selection of candidate R&D projects? Did market analysis inform the process of research execution and prototype design? If so, how?

- Were technical, political, financial, and institutional barriers to prototype adoption anticipated? Was the technology development path adjusted to match the dynamics of the delivery system?

- Was market adoption considered a measure of project success? Was "proof of concept" or "proof of sales" the intended end point of the research, development, and demonstration process?

- Was overt supplier or consumer resistance a primary cause of implementation failure, indicating the need for market-making strategies such as tax subsidies or surtaxes or more forceful political commitment to the enforcement of standards?

The studies were conducted through a review of project documents—articles that could be found in the trade and technical journals—and interviews with project managers and technical personnel. Most of the interviews were conducted in person. Interviewees were selected for a range of policy levels and technical viewpoints. Emphasis was placed on market adoption and diffusion as primary measures of project success.

The analysis yielded a number of generalizations about the reasons for the failure of federal research, development, and demonstration programs to produce technologies that fit market needs in local government and the private sector. These generalizations are supportive of the hypothesis that implementation failure is a function of "policy push and market pull." The study found four important causes of implementation failure:

- Inadequate attention to problem definition, needs analysis, and market matching

- Program continuity insufficient to permit development of the agency and supplier and market link necessary for the adoption and diffusion of innovations

- Excessively costly technologies

- Conflict between the public interest and the goals of the technology delivery system

• Insufficient effort to anticipate barriers to implementation

The hypothesis can therefore be restated as propositions that seek to explain the high failure rate of federally funded research, development, and demonstration:

• Research, development, and demonstration teams have displayed a bias toward purely physical solutions; as a consequence, "needs" have been defined in terms of technological systems rather than in terms of fitting physical components into existing sociotechnical systems.

• Project success has not been measured by technology adoption and diffusion; in fact, the regard and prestige structure of R&D agencies is still not tied to the success of implementation, but to reputation-makers such as size of budget, size of project, technical elegance of approach, and challenge of research problem.

• Self-serving political demands can distort a project budget, timetable, and demonstration site in a fashion that distracts the project team from its concern with engineering performance or market impact.

• There is a general lack of market information and marketing savvy in the federal R&D establishment. Because market analysis is not conducted early in the R&D process, it does not seem to influence the screening of candidate technologies. Similarly, cost analysis does not seem to be conducted in time to abort projects that are certain or probable losers. This is part and parcel of the technologist's belief that "implementation is somebody else's problem."

• Program continuity, in terms of personnel, funding levels, and policy priorities, is lacking. It is necessary for developing the constellation of suppliers, developers, and return customers that makes up a mature technology delivery system.

• Agencies with R&D missions often are not equipped with implementation authority. Intervention efforts necessary to motivate the technology delivery system often are lacking.

• The failure often is a function of the shortcomings of standard-setting as an incentive for innovation. Where market processes do not produce socially desirable results, the conventional federal approach has been to impose regulations.

• Efforts are undertaken in a context framed by economic and ideological conventions about the appropriate rules of the public and private sectors.

Proposed Solutions

The failure of the federal R&D management process to consider implementation issues during the design stage has rendered it ineffectual in dealing with the market or political demands initially prompting program authorization. To resolve the problem, an approach can be taken that is sensitive to the differences between the sectors rather than one that is eager to make the federal research agencies operate like private industry. This strategy—the Technology Implementation Plan—incorporates such considerations as the end user, the supply system, technical feasibility, cost and marketing, and barriers, into technology selection, project specification, program monitoring, and budget decisions—the research management process.[19]

The Technology Implementation Plan is an explicit procedure that considers documents, and monitors the probability of implementation success. It is a strategic planning and research activity intended for incorporation in the annual cycle of program budgeting and the day-to-day activities of the research process.

The Plan is designed for application at the program level, where go/no-go and increase/decrease decisions about technology development budgets are made. It involves a continuing process of technology assessment based on implementation feasibility. The application of the Plan at the program level is intended to lodge responsibility for considering implementation with the program manager rather than with the technical specialist. It requires that the program manager coordinate with staff technologists regarding questions of technical feasibility, market acceptance, and implementation strategy.

Such an information form serves to define the implementation path of a candidate technology and helps anticipate potential barriers. Consequently, the research plan will include strategies for relaxing barriers to implementation through design improvements, regulatory strategies, or subsidy measures.

The Technology Implementation Plan is designed to help the program manager reevaluate the merits of technology systems each year as more conclusive information on performance, cost, and implementation barriers becomes available. Thus, it demands that the program manager work with staff technologists to develop evaluation "milestones" that stress not only technical feasibility but also market acceptance and implementation. The milestones are designed for incorporation as an integral element of the annual review cycle and allow a form of Zero-Based Budgeting in the selection of R&D priorities.

To institutionalize such a system as the Technology Implementation Plan, it is important to realize that it represents fundamental changes in the structure of public sector R&D agencies. The first change is organizational and requires that the persons responsible for monitoring a program be capable of evaluating both its technical and its marketing aspects. Presently, good public R&D managers are people who are technically competent; often they are researchers themselves, attend professional meetings, give papers, and publish articles and books. The proclivity of such people is to do and sponsor research that will further develop the state of technical understanding. This motivates researchers, as we have already noted, to prove concepts rather than respond to problems. Some federal R&D managers are engineers, trained as problem solvers and capable of evaluating the technical work of projects. Most of them, however, are not interested in, or qualified to assess, the effective demand for the new knowledge or resultant technology in the marketplace. Management specialists in R&D positions have the obvious problem of not being able to evaluate and monitor the technical portions of the program. An ideal solution would be to hire people who are not only skilled in the technical aspects of the program, but also have had real-world marketing experience. Such people are not readily available, and those that have such talents are often reluctant to leave lucrative positions in private industry. In the interim, some reliance could be put on teams of people who are willing to trade off their technical and marketing experiences with each other.

A second change is attitudinal and requires a noticeable shift in the R&D reward structure. Most people are willing to agree to a reasonable, clearly defined goal as long as the goal was recognized by their superiors. This means that the Technology Implementation Plan and its stress on end users has to be supported by people in positions of authority. It would help if all levels of an administration endorsed the Plan, because each level would support the one below it, such that the whole philosophy of research management responsibility would be established. For project managers, though, all that is required is that their managers support the Technology Implementation Plan concept and make clear how it will be used to rank projects and judge personnel for advancement.

The suggested solution to the problems of implementing technology types of project would not work in exactly the same way as transferring, say, health-related research results to the policy areas, where health-based standards must be set for regulatory purposes.

The notion of fundamental differences in how people in the public and private sectors approach their professions has permitted development of a method that recognizes these differences and takes them into account explicitly. In the next chapter we shall take a similar look at the worlds of the scientist and analyst to see if they are fundamentally different, as the federal and private-sector research managers were different, and, if they are, whether the differences account for information transfer difficulties and, if so, whether they can be overcome.

NOTES AND REFERENCES

1.   National Archives Records Service, General Services Administration, *U.S. Government Manual*, U.S. Government Printing Office, Washington, D.C., May 1980.

2.   Organization of Economic Co-Operation and Development, *Management of Research and Development*, Istanbul, Turkey.

3.   Michael Reagan, *Science and the Federal Patron*, Oxford University Press, New York, 1969, p. 36.

4.   J. Wert, A. Lieberman, and R. Levian, *R&D Management. Methods Used by Federal Agencies*, Lexington Books, D. C. Heath and Company, Lexington, Massachusetts, 1975.

5.   Ibid.

6.   R. O. Mason, "The Role of Management in Science," *Public Administration Review*, Mar/Apr 1979.

7.   A recent law, the Stevenson-Wydler Technology Innovation Act of 1980, was designed specifically to enhance the utility of public sector research through technology transfer.

8.   The market-demand orientation of much industrial research was demonstrated empirically in Jacob Schmookler's classic book, *The Sources of Invention*, Harvard University Press, Cambridge, Massachusetts, 1966.

9.   Daniel D. Roman, *Science, Technology, and Innovation*, Grid Publishing Company, Columbus, Ohio, 1980, pp. 418–420.

10.   This standard of success is so important to companies that a considerable amount of effort goes into trying to forecast which projects will yield an adequate return. Ansoff, for example, has devised a complex formula for estimating the merit (profit) of a proposed project. I. H. Ansoff, "Evaluation of Applied Research in a Business Firm," in J. R. Bright, (Ed.), *Research, Development and Technological Innovation*, Richard Irwin, Homewood, Illinois, 1964, pp. 468–480. Many other schemata exist as well. See Brian Twiss, *Managing Technological Innovation*, Longman Group Ltd., London, 1974, Chap. 6.

11.   Sumner Myers and Eldon E. Sweezy, "Why Innovations Fail," *Technology Review,* Vol. 80, March/April 1978, pp. 41–46.

12.   This "defensive" strategy generally emphasizes the development end of the research and development continuum. Brian Twiss, *Managing Technological Innovation,* Longman Group Ltd., London, 1974, p. 58.

13.   Greenberg's account of science and technology policy-making in the United States gives an excellent, although somewhat dated, view of the complex struggles involved in hammering out policy stands. Daniel S. Greenberg, World Publishing Company, New York, 1967.

14.   Eric A. von Hippel, "Users as Innovators," *Technology Review,* Vol. 80, January 1978, pp. 31–39.

15.   Probably the best known example of such market incompatibility was Du Pont's costly development and marketing of Corfam. Edwin A. Gee and Chaplin Tyler, *Managing Innovation,* Wiley, New York, 1978, p. 34. Another is the ill-fated Edsel.

16.   J. Herbert Hollomon et al., *Government Involvement in the Innovation Process,* Office of Technology Assessment, Washington, D.C., 1978, p. 54.

17.   Peter W. House and David W. Jones, *Getting It Off the Shelf, A Methodology for Implementing Federal Research,* Westview Press, Boulder, Colorado, 1976, pp. 185–192.

18.   *Ibid.*

19.   *Ibid.,* pp. 256–280.

CHAPTER 3
Cast of Characters

Policy research is restricted to those branches of the science community concerned with knowledge, ideas, findings—information, as opposed to physical products. The applied research, analysis, and assessment communities are perceived as the groups that incorporate the basic-research results with other information into products for public and private sector decisions. In the last chapter we showed that, for those portions of the science community that have as their output physical products, there is a defined literature that goes under the rubric of "technology transfer." To the extent that this literature has matured into an understanding of how one moves new hardware research and development products from one sector to another, the methods and solutions used in transferring products and techniques between sectors might be useful in accomplishing a similar transfer of ideas and information from the science community to the regulatory and policy streams.

The issue of concern revolves about the question of how to transfer the latest scientific information to the policy level in a timely and efficient manner. To date, transfer institutions have not worked well because their conceptualization or implementation of their mission was flawed or did not have the reward structure or incentive for enticing them to fulfill the function.

We have essentially "shot the messenger." Intensive studies of the transfer of scientific information to another professional community, as we noted above, have not changed attitudes, because no one wanted, or understood how, to effect such a transfer. The training and professional biases of the responsible program manager tended to produce programs unrealistic in terms of information transfer. The difficulties with these transfer attempts lay not in the formal mechanisms developed but in the personal and institutional approaches taken. Realizing this, we believe that by understanding more about the "actors" we may be able to discover more realistic and effective management and transfer mechanisms.

In this examination we develop a generic perspective for each of these professions and determine their similarities and differences. Later, on the basis of the insights gained, we discuss ways that information, findings, or needs might be moved more efficiently and effectively from the science community to the policy analyst or executive—the areas of most interest to us here.

The research scientist is often pictured as unique, with his own set of goals, beliefs, and prejudices. In fact this may or may not really be true or, in any case, necessary, for the proper performance of his job. But to the extent that the science profession is unique among all professions, or is perceived as such by its members or those who interact with them, a potential for misunderstanding is set in place that cannot help affecting the science product and its acceptance. To illustrate this difficulty, we look at three stylized comparisons, between (1) the scientist and the marketing group, (2) the scientist and the administrator, and (3) the scientist and the policy analyst. The first two comparisons are cursory and depend heavily on other sources. The last, because it is of more direct importance for us here, is more fully developed.

THE SCIENTIST

Throughout history, to label someone a scientist has been to speak in honorific terms. Although some scientists have at times been less than honored because of their discipline or its application (e.g., military scientists in times of peace), science has generally been a prestigious profession. It embodies many specific disciplines, cuts across all geopolitical boundaries, and has a common language and approach. Its universality is a major quality in the scientific community.[1]

Let us now turn to an examination of some of the more prominent attributes of the fellowship of science, using the framework mentioned above. In doing so we should keep in mind that we are searching for an understanding of the essence of this fellowship—the motivations behind its unique properties, its opportunities and ability to interact with others, and the utility to society of its findings.

Tradition

A fellowship of scientists has existed for hundreds of years across a variety of cultures. Examples of this tradition or club or fraternity are without regard to the political stances of any parent country. It exists around the world, being membered by representatives of most countries. It is even posited that science is by and large above politics. Capitalizing on this belief, former President Johnson approached McGeorge Bundy, head of the Ford Foundation, and encouraged him to create an international organization that would permit communication between nations even when they were in formal disagreement (at that time, the United States and the Soviet Union). The resulting organization was the International Institute for Applied Systems Analysis in Laxenburg, Austria.[2] Others are the International Council of Scientific Unions and its associate unions, which respectively cover astronomy, biochemistry, biological sciences, pure and applied chemistry, crystallography, geodesy and geophysics, geography, history and philosophy of science, physiological sciences, pure and applied physics, radio science, theoretical and applied mechanics, geological sciences, pure and applied biophysics, nutritional sciences, pharmacology, and immunological societies.[3]

Other examples of the tradition, such as formalized clubs and societies for the scientific élite, are replicated in country after country. In 1893 the Congress chartered the National Academy of Sciences, giving it the responsibility to "investigate, experiment, and report" on scientific subjects "whenever called upon by any department of the Government." This institution is now the ranking organization of United States science; the number of new members admitted yearly is limited to 35 Americans and four foreigners, all chosen for their achievements in basic research. Thus, this group is not only an honor society for those who have made outstanding contributions to science, but also an advisory and oversight body that is often asked to help with quality control or mediate issues between groups.[4]

Methodology

Nearly every introductory textbook in the physical sciences sets out the basic, universal rules for carrying out scientific research. The scientific method embodies a high degree of precision in the language used in scientific descriptions and explanations. New work is introduced by defining it in terms already in use. When possible, concepts are defined in quantitative terms, and the personal and emotional associations that individuals attach to certain concepts are excluded. The approach relies on a strict application of formal logic and proceeds by a series of steps, which might be presented as follows.

- Stating the hypothesis: A potentially correct explanation of a phenomenon is offered, which orients the investigation to specific subjects and disciplines.

- Gathering information: The scientist acquires definitive information that reveals possible relationships among various factors and elements of the hypothesis.

- Making preliminary observations: With the knowledge gained in the previous step, an experiment or test is designed to prove or disprove the hypothesis by means of "controlled" experimentation.

- Performing controlled experiments: In many cases available and current knowledge on the subject matter of the hypothesis is insufficient for testing, confirming, or disproving the hypothesis; additional data must be obtained through controlled experiments.

- Classifying experimental data: Information pertaining to the problem is sorted and the interpretation of the data delineated. In some cases a tentative conclusion is easy to discern, while in others it is extremely difficult. Inductive and deductive reasoning both come into play in this step.

- Testing the conclusion: This is one of the most important steps in the scientific method. If the investigation has been thorough, the tentative conclusion should support or disprove the stated hypothesis. It should be able to be tested by others, who will actually perform the same experiment under the same prescribed conditions.

- Adjusting the hypothesis: Sometimes the tentative conclusion, and therefore the stated hypothesis, requires revision. In this situation the process is repeated, beginning with the revised stated hypothesis.

These rules are expected to be followed by every operating scientist because they are agreed upon by the scientific community as both the ideal and actual approach that every research effort should follow. It is likely, however, that they are more often rigidly honored in the presentation of the results than in the actual research. Further, they are better applied to the physical sciences, such as chemistry and physics, where the laws of natural phenomena are studied, than to the social and economic sciences, in which attitudes and practices sometimes change or are subject to interpretation. Nonetheless, in general the method is held to be valid by everyone who goes by the name "scientist," regardless of geographic location or discipline.

Characteristically, within any particular subcategory of science is a widely recognized core of knowledge[5]—although this tends to be less true as the "frontiers" of knowledge are approached. This body of knowledge is sufficiently well categorized for a student to feel reasonably comfortable studying the basics of a particular field of science almost anywhere in the world and moving to a university in another nation to continue his education. Most people in a particular scientific discipline can be expected to have the same set of skills and basic information irrespective of the location of their schooling.[6] It is only in graduate school, where specialization and research are more of a factor in the education process, that the homogenization of information is less certain.

This consistency makes for great efficiency in adding to the base of knowledge as the base, coupled with the peer review process, builds and shifts more or less uniformly everywhere. If the sciences are going to treat their base of information (and the methods used to generate that information) as valid, then an obvious requirement of a piece of research in any branch of science is that anyone else trained in that branch be able to replicate it.[7]

All of these features of the science paradigm are related in the sense that they tend to "dehumanize" the scientist. Flashes of brilliance are treated with suspicion in fields where almost everyone is intellectually very bright and where care and rigor are important traits. Precision and care and record-keeping and checking and re-checking are the rule—often plodding work.[8]

In fact, the real world is not so neat and tidy as these principles of basic science would suggest. In some fields, as already noted, the principles would be more or less accurate; in others, less so. Most science managers and those responsible for funding research, however, might agree that it would be difficult to fund research that did not at least pay lip service to the formal scientific method, or to fund individuals or groups who did not professedly adhere to them. On the other hand, there is strong suspicion that it may be possible to obtain research results faster than under the science model just out-lined by, say, increasing expenditures in some area, shifting the re-sources focused on a problem, or short-circuiting the standard research structure.[9] As to the last, some might argue that an accelerated re-search strategy would increase the risk that an "incorrect" finding were used in a policy decision, or that the most "important" finding, from a scientific perspective, would not be addressed.[10] Further, there is a cynical suspicion that throwing money at a problem doesn't guar-antee success or a solution, and that the legitimate area for such research is in applied science, not basic.

In sum, the average scientist is trained to be conservative in his profession. He is trained in a formal logic and proceeds to "solve" a problem with the general feeling that he has to know "everything" about a specific issue, before he is willing to say anything definitive about it. He expects to be in control of his analysis, from data to techniques to final presentation.

Timing

The slow, deliberate pace suggested by these customs of science leads directly to the observation that change in what is "known" in a scientific sense is augmented carefully and incrementally. Seldom is it expected that one scientist, or even a group of scientists, will make a revolutionary breakthrough. Most of those that do are rewarded by Nobel prizes. Many of the more recent leaps are not really breakthroughs in the classic sense but have been confirmatory in nature and have come to pass with the aid of impressive additions to the scientist's research kit bag in the form of technical hardware (for example, electron microscopes and computers). "Confirmatory" means that long-held suspicions are being sustained or disproved, not through new insights but by measurement techniques, for example, that have enabled expanded investigation.[11]

In the main, though, most scientists at the working level zero in on the same fairly specific items, which they study and restudy and check to ensure that their results will be judged additions to the knowledge base—new and necessarily accurate. It is these small and clearly discrete projects, pursued under agreed-upon rules and with a maximum of communication among colleagues, that allow orderly progress in our scientific knowledge.

Resources

Scientists receive money from the government for two main purposes: to add to the knowledge base and to resolve uncertainty and lack of understanding regarding operational or technical issues. For the first—basic science—research is not normally undertaken to produce a specific product. This differs from the second, which is typically applied research. Both may be a part of the legitimate funding purview of a mission agency, though it is the latter that is the more often discussed in this regard.

From a scientist's perspective, there never seem to be adequate resources to answer the questions at the frontier of scientific knowledge that are characteristic of basic research.[12] On the other hand, the ability of a given scientific discipline to advance the state of knowledge sometimes depends on the availability of talented scientists and the complexity of the questions. For example, despite extensive funding of research in fusion energy since the nineteen-fifties, that science is not seen to be practically available until 2020 or so. The mere desire on the part of society to "solve" a problem or the decision to spend large sums of research money in some area may be a necessary, but often is not a sufficient, condition of success.

Personnel

The scientific community has its own training grounds where its disciplines and traditions are most prominently promoted: universities. In the view of some the professors in these institutions act the role of priests and the students their pedagogical disciples. In many cases the purpose of the institution is to move the novices through the indoctrination process and various stages: undergraduate to graduate students, to postdoctoral candidates, to professors or research scientists. To return to a university and attain the position of full professor—a high priest of science—is the traditional goal in the fellowship of science.[13]

Quality

In its purest form science is able to be practiced by those adequately trained in its rigors, regardless of whether a particular scientist is widely recognized already or is just beginning a career. In other words, previous recognition or reputation is, ideally, not expected to be a factor in whether the research results are acceptable or not: the quality or utility of the research should be based on the merits of the argument alone.[14] To facilitate this, several safeguards are taken; for example, papers submitted for publication in professional journals are referred to reviewers who are anonymous to the authors.

Another type of peer review consists of reviewing a program (or programs) of scientist (or group of scientists), as opposed to reviewing the findings of one project. Such reviews are normally performed by a collection of recognized scientists, trained in performing similar research, and sitting as judges to ensure quality. Finally, these same peer groups might participate in the design of new efforts in specific areas; or, alternatively, these efforts are often accomplished by convening groups of selected scientists under the aegis of scientific organizations such as the National Academy of Sciences. These same organizationally sponsored groups might also carry out program reviews.

Such types of peer review are made possible by the understanding that there is a current body of knowledge agreed upon by all the savants in the field. The purpose of the peer review is to ensure general agreement that the new information is a meaningful addition to the discipline's information base.

Clients

The customers for the findings of basic research are other scientists. These scientists will use the new information to formulate hypotheses in turn, which they will test in the search for new insights into the physical laws of nature. On the other hand, the customers for applied research are engineers and decision-makers, who will use the new knowledge to design improved hardware or to decide on the feasibility or efficacy of proceeding with certain projects or programs or setting regulations at certain levels.[15]

Clients of the basic-science community do not normally influence the methods employed or the findings obtained. If they do, then it is in taking care that the scientific method was followed and that the peer review system was used. Serious tampering with the process or personnel usually results in discrediting both the scientist and his findings.[16]

The picture of science as neat and orderly in the way it carries out its business is, of course, a blown-up one. On the other hand, the general trend set by such a philosophy is a spiritual support to how a scientist idealizes his profession. It does not explain revolutionary additions to the knowledge base, which are often made by people of genius, or accidental discoveries. But again, for our purposes, the important issue is the self-image of the practitioners, or the image some have of them, not the actual functioning personality.

With these generalizations about scientists in mind, we shall now contrast them with other equally stereotyped professionals, who concern us here and who are associated with scientists in their day-to-day operations. First, marketers.

THE SCIENTIST AND THE MARKETER

Just what research is done in the private sector (as we saw in the previous chapter) ultimately depends largely on people's wanting to buy the products the research produces. Except in the rarest of cases, this does not happen automatically but is the result of positive action on the part of a company to sell each newly produced product. As noted earlier, the selling is most difficult to accomplish after the research is done—especially if it was done with no market in mind. It is a marginal matter at best, and often impossible, to sell solid gold Cadillacs if the public wants Volkswagen Rabbits. To minimize the frustration of marketing departments that are expected to move already developed but poorly conceived research losers, the most obvious solution would be to have the marketer and the scientist interact early and often. But this has historically proved difficult. In a study of 38 industrial research firms[17] four typical scientist-marketer interface problems were identified: lack of communication, lack of appreciation, distrust, and personal friendships. These four problems were discussed in terms of the typical behavior and attitudes of the two groups.

Lack of communication

- Behavior: Some difficulties were too few joint meetings and not enough cross-attendance at each others' staff meetings; neither group kept the other routinely informed of its own activities.

- Attitudes: Both groups felt that it was not useful to become very involved with the details of what the other does.

Lack of appreciation

- Behavior: The research and development department sometimes attempted to market its own ideas, or it failed to use the in-house expertise available; or Marketing contracted out for its R&D needs.

- Attitudes: Marketing felt that R&D was too sophisiticated and talked over clients' heads; R&D felt that Marketing was too simplistic in its approaches and did not really understand what products were needed.

Distrust

- Behavior: Marketing tended to dominate what was needed and how to produce it; no room was left for rebuttal.

- Attitudes: Marketing felt that R&D could not be trusted either to make known to the outside what was being developed or to keep the inside apprised of progress until a product appeared— and that the product was often not what was wanted; R&D felt muzzled and threatened, and distrusted Marketing's ability to know what the client wanted.

Personal friendships

- Behavior: Both parties avoided conflict and were socially friendly; potential problems were glossed over.

- Attitudes: Neither wanted to hurt the other and did not compete; each had a high regard for the other.

The article goes on to suggest a number of ways that problems in these areas might be mitigated. For our purposes this discussion is not necessary, as we are more interested in the interactions between scientists and policy analysts. The study is an example, however, of the "we-they" syndrome that develops between professional groups.

THE SCIENTIST AND THE ADMINISTRATOR

In the private sector a smooth relationship between the research and marketing divisions of a firm is obviously important. In both the public and private sectors similar relationships are necessary between the scientist and the administrator. Although it sometimes happens that scientists and researchers become marketers (or analysts), they more often become administrators. As such, they assume a dichotomous thinking, part of it having been fostered early by professional preparation in the academic community, which makes the transition difficult for them. There is customarily little in the way of formal training in administration for science or science in administration. One finds a general feeling that anybody can run a program. In fact, in the science community, those who give up research and become program managers (or public bureaucrats who caretake the funds of research) are sometimes considered to be those who no longer are able to be scientists or proved to be second-rate ones. Still other scientist-managers are promoted to management positions as a reward for good science. This is a classic example of the Peter Principle[18] in which a highly competent performer in one area of expertise will get promoted to another—and prove incompetent. A lack of respect for, or understanding of the need of, good manangement does not help in learning the skills of that specialty and may mean that a scientist never becomes an accomplished manager.

The truth is, once again, that managers and scientists are trained in their own specialties and that the methods and techniques and even the ethos each develops are characteristically different for each. Both are legitimate, however, in that they serve their own purposes. Recently Sauder provided a brief synopsis of science and management:[19]

> Scientists and engineers are trained and sensitized to use methodical logic and objective thinking. They are trained to make conclusions and solve problems through the application of theorems and proofs. They are taught to seek unequivocal evidence before coming to a final conclusion. The formal training of a scientist or an engineer emphasizes an analytical capability and

the scientific approach. The focus is on finding exact solutions to well-defined problems, by the use of objective data and established theories. Sound technical decision making depends on the ability to apply rigorous methods of searching out causes and solutions to problems.

By contrast, managerial decision making requires an ability to size up people and situations, with only a minimum of information about symptoms. An effective manager is able to diagnose a situation when only a very small amount of the problem iceberg is visible. This is in direct contrast to the scientific approach. The scientific approach to decision making uses a large volume of well-ordered information, which is sifted and evaluated in the light of established theories and concepts. By contrast, the manager may modify the theory with each new problem. Management theories are often nebulous and tentative, and are often based on a few individual cases. In effect, the manager has relatively few established rules and principles to rely on.

The author contends that these different skills are not easily acquired and that successful change between the roles is often difficult. But the movement is commonplace. Why?

Reasons vary, but they generally are attributable to such factors as that the career ladders in many of the public and private sectors, including science, are relatively limited, and an individual interested in personal advancement will typically find it necessary to take on administrative duties. In the science area, responsible management of many of the more esoteric programs requires knowledge of the field for making intelligent decisions. Further, once the use of trained technical specialists becomes established, there is a tendency to perpetuate the practice. People who do the hiring feel comfortable with people who speak the same language. To the extent that the hirings in the public sector are responsive to external pressure, there is an expectation that scientists will lobby for other scientists to fill the administrative positions, adding still another form of pressure to the hiring practices.

The fact remains, however, that there is no correlation between being a good (or even great) scientist and being a good (or even adequate) manager. The suggestion that managers and marketers on the one hand and scientists on the other appreciate each other's tasks and can even assume each other's roles is partially realized by their having at least a conceptual understanding of each other's function.

In our attempt to understand why scientists and administrators act the way they do toward each other we employed the perspective of the scientist and the government administrator. The stereotype of public actors is important since, as we have already discussed, it is they who ultimately decide which research is funded, the funding levels, and the project's success. Kiren highlights three aspects:[20]

- Facts: The scientist is seen as a person who is very precise about what is or is not a fact, the government person, under pressure to make a decision, decides when there is enough information to reduce the risk of a decision to its minimum and then deals as if he had a valid fact (as opposed to a hypothesis).

- Problem-solving: The task of the scientist is to search for solutions, or at least to understand more and more about an issue so that eventually a puzzle can be solved. Government persons are not so sanguine about ever really "solving" a problem; their skills are compromise and accommodation. Even more to the point, analysts characteristically deal with issues that are not usually thought of as something to be "solved."

- Values: Government people operate in a world where values are one of the realities of politics; interest groups and individual perspectives are a part of their everyday life. The scientist, in his world of facts, moves value-free, or at least tries to.

These extreme postures are not meant to have the connotation of "good" or "bad." They are stereotypes, however, that are held by many who attempt to interface the public-sector funding community with the scientific community.

For our purposes, each of the comparisons so far has demonstrated that the way the scientist looks at the world is different from the way other professionals do. However, each perspective is legitimate and is designed to enable each of the professions to do its job most effectively by focusing on a limited set of facets of any given issue. The last comparison, the scientist and the analyst, is the one which is the most important for our work. We have designed our discussion of their characteristics so that the categories are the same as those used earlier for the scientist; see also Table 1.

THE SCIENTIST AND THE POLICY ANALYST

Since the discipline of policy analysis is relatively new, there may be many different notions about the role such persons play in carrying out their analyses. Therefore, a short introductory section is deemed appropriate before elaborating on the policy analyst stereotype.

Policy analysts are found in all levels of government, in special-interest groups, and in private industry. In the following dissertation

Table 1
Science and Assessment Paradigm's Characteristics

Science	Assessment
Tradition:	
Fraternal organizations, societies	Recognition
Methodology:	
Scientific method	Varied methodologies
Established knowledge base	Lack of universal knowledge base
Timing:	
Slow, incremental change	Restrictive
Confirmatory discoveries	"Brushfire"
Resources:	
Reflect problem complexity	Inadequate levels
Personnel:	
Channeled training	Generalists
Quality:	
Peer review	Subjective objectivity
Clients:	
Scientists, engineers, decision-makers	Decision-makers
Objective	Decision-maker influences

"policy" means a guiding principle of an organization. For example, the Reagan Administration was dedicated to reducing federal expenditures generally and reducing the federal regulatory burden (getting the government "off our backs"). The Department of Energy under Reagan shifted its research and development policy from "commercialization" of near-term technologies to "long-term high-risk" research. An environmental-interest group might have a policy to "keep the pressure on" the federal regulators. A large corporation might have an environmental policy that acquiesced to all new regulations except those that were blatantly wasteful in terms of cost effectiveness.

The policy analyst does not select, or promulgate, the policies—that is the purview of the politician or senior executive of the institution. The policy analyst advises the policy-maker of the past, present, and likely future impacts and effects of a given policy or a set of alternative new policies, so that the policy-maker can pursue the most advantageous path from his point of view. To be of utmost use, the analysis must include the physical, demographic, economic, institutional, and political impacts. Policy analyses have become institutionalized now, in such forms as the Environmental Impact Statement and the Regulatory Impact Analysis. Because of the broad range of topics that must be covered, journeymen and senior policy analysts become highly interdisciplinary individuals, developing (at least superficially) the skills and working knowledge of many different professions.

Extensive studies of the proposed impacts of policies or actions are frequently termed "assessments." In this discussion the terms "analysis" and "assessment" are more or less interchangeable, although the latter implies greater rigor and quantification. Policy analysts usually deal with "issues"—discrete situations or occurrences that arise and require interpretation in the context of existing policies or development of new policies. In a working sense, "issue" is synonomous with "topic," "problem," or "task" for the policy analyst.

If one were to put together a stereotype of the analytic community, the typical analyst would seem to be the opposite of the scientist. He is given questions that he must answer as best he can, and so specializes in formulating these questions into issues that may be addressed with available data and information. (These are to be distinguished from the hypotheses of the scientist, which are to be "tested" for correctness.) The analyst's job is to provide a quality response to an issue, given available time and resources. It is an art more than a technique, in which the possible is separated from the unguessable as expeditiously as possible. To some extent the analyst may be seen as addressing only portions of a particular question, and these portions are decided by available information and the situation in which the analysis is being done.

In no way is this process to be visualized as a search for basic knowledge; rather, it is a search for alternative responses to questions embedded in the context of the "current situation." To some extent the situation of the policy analyst parallels that of the engineer, who is expected to do the best he can, given a specific time period and defined resources.

Our stylization of the scientist was, to some extent, easier to fabricate than that of the professional who performs assessments or analyses for regulatory or other purposes. The broad-brush treatment we gave of the stereotypical scientist included impressions that this group might have of themselves as well as characteristics attributed to them by others. Clearly, no one would hold all these impressions at all times. The descriptions used were apt to engender both agreement and disagreement as to accuracy, depending upon the reader. The point to be made, though, is not whether everyone can agree on all of the stereotypes (clearly impossible), but that the term "science" evokes a mental image of certain behavior on the part of a practitioner, even though this image may not be perfectly consistent from one person to the next.

The person engaged in analysis or assessment is not as easy to categorize or generalize as the scientist. One might, however, say that scientists tend to deal with highly specialized subject matter (specialists), whereas analysts tend to deal with more comprehensive and broader issues (generalists). Although the analyst is not in any way better or worse than the scientist, he is clearly a different animal. The descriptions attempted below will reflect this lack of concreteness and, in several cases, resort to a discussion of what an analyst is not, rather than of what the practice of analysis is. The reader is explicitly admonished once again, however, that these two professions and their practitioners are in no way "better," the one than the other. It should become obvious, though, that they are different, and each unique. For our purposes, this is all that is important to convey. The following sections discuss some of the general features of the analysis-assessment model, using the same general categories as those used for the scientist. Because they are directly germane to the subject of managing applied science in the public sector, especially in the regulatory areas, we shall handle this stereotype much as we did that of the scientist.

Tradition

The assessment of issues and policies is a relatively new formal discipline, derived to a large extent from the application of such analytic techniques as cost–benefit or cost-effectiveness analysis, or others found in systems analysis, applied science, and operations research. In its early stages such practices were thought by the technical community to be basic-science castoffs, unable to make a go of it in specialized disciplines and therefore resigned to dealing in generalities. It has only been since World War II that professional training and societies relating to the assessment discipline have been widely recognized. Because the issues with which the analyst must deal are closely tied to political and upper-management decision-making, they are constantly changing in character and importance. As a result the discipline lacks a universal knowledge base that can be expanded, as in the sciences (although the information available in basic science is often mined by the applied scientist). Methodology is usually the only common element in the assessment discipline. The limits of analysis and assessment are often not easily recognized by the users of the results (who normally expect too much too soon) and sometimes not by the practitioners (who have been known to promise more than they can deliver). As yet there is no effective self-policing mechanism for the professional field of analysis and assessment as there is for science. The results are often based on judgment, not peer-reviewed "truth."

Methodology

The goal of the analyst is not "truth" but policy information with insight. The approach commonly used in assessment is to break issues into their components for further examination of their parts. By this means the alternatives for resolving the issues are studied, and where possible a quantification of the issues' elements is attempted. Often data and information initially obtained by others (such as scientists) are used in the analysis. Some relatively rigorous research, however, may be needed, to give insights and establish relationships not immediately obvious in a complex issue. In the assessment discipline the problems addressed are generally messy, ill defined, and not well bounded. To some extent this causes difficulty for the practitioners, who often rely on fairly rigorous analytic tools to carry out their work. Such an approach differs from systems analysis and operations research, which work best when the system to be analyzed is well bounded. The applied researcher-analyst has to produce the best results possible, given resource and information constraints. The performance of this type of work means creativity in the design of the analysis and caveats in the results.

Timing

The policy analyst normally operates under a tyranny of time. He refers to the situation in which "the policy window is open," meaning that although he may be intellectually in favor of carrying out more traditional research, the realities of the situation do not allow it. On issues worthy of investigation a decision will be made about whether or not an analyst can complete a first-rate assessment. An obvious and immutable rule for an effective policy group is that any analysis of a proposed action must be ready before the final policy decision is made.

Consequently, issues that are complex but have little time for examination may get analyses whose reliability is easily open to question. Even so, the analyses should be the best possible under the circumstances. If an analysis is periodically revised, analytical tools may be expected to lead to more reliable results, allow shorter turnaround time, and yield more comprehensive and sophisticated analysis.

The realities of public policy analysis mean that analysts must constantly deal with "brushfire" issues. The actual day-to-day job consists of responding to crises—real or imagined—that are important to a policy-maker. Usually it is a pick-and shovel job and often requires little more than a telephone call or two to verify a situation, gather data, and prepare the informative issue paper or response.

The highly sophisticated, technically demanding, event-shaping analysis so often discussed in the literature arises only a few times each year. But it appears often enough to challenge the more creative of the analysts on the effective public policy staffs.

Those who perform assessments and other workers in applied research feel the stricture of time but normally not to the same degree as the public policy analyst. To their opposites in the basic-science community they seem under an inordinate pressure of time; to the analysts, the pace seems positively leisurely.

Resources

Certainly, a question of the appropriate criteria for welfare eligibility can hardly be expected to be analyzed with the same resources and fervor as the question of a revised budget for a minor government unit. Although this comparison is extreme, it does remind us that most public decisions may be regarded as policy or as a basis for policy formulation. More sophisticated and complex methodologies and analyses are required for the more difficult policy decisions. The matching of issues and resources is often a complex task even for those experienced in analysis. Preliminary screening and a consideration of the alternatives usually take place before significant resources are devoted to an analysis.

Just as little time may be available for an analysis, so too the resources to carry it out may be limited. It might be hypothesized that the government should allocate resource levels that are appropriate to the value of the policy decision at hand. This could mean that millions of taxpayer dollars should be spent for some public policy analyses. The vagaries of the political process, however, often make it difficult to allocate adequate resources to the variety of proposed policies, particularly since the budget process would require that such funds be set aside for as long as a year before they are actually needed for any policy analyses. In reality, truly adequate funds are rarely available, but analyses are delivered anyway. On the other hand, critics of formal analysis, as of scientific research, tend to question the high cost of the work compared with the results produced. Perhaps hindsight analysis is useful, in that future planning efforts for analysis or research might include more awareness of the potential for waste.

The resources available for applied research are similarly constrained; there never appears to be enough time, given the demand for the output. In the case of assessments, because the time period for production is longer, the potential for wasting the science resources is greater. It takes a lot of management skill (and not a little luck) to have an assessment product on hand just when it is needed—for the setting of a regulation or as input into a policy.

Personnel

Probably the rarest commodity in any policy shop is talent—the talent to perform sophisticated, balanced, insightful analyses under extreme pressures and usually in a short time. Talented analysts get to the heart of an issue quickly. Because of familiarity with general issues, they can usually relate a current issue to others in the policy stream at that moment. In addition to their technical skills and political sense, analysts rely to some extent on their share of luck, given the uncertainties of the political process. Whatever the elusive components of such a talent, policy analysts are difficult to find, train, and keep sufficiently challenged for long periods of time.

In the average policy shop, where the tasks are numerous and usually of high priority with short time fuses, there is often an imbalance between jobs to be done and people to do them. Besides the number of tasks that are assigned, a complicating factor is the variety of approaches needed to dispose of the broad set of tasks. A query may be handled by the analyst's spending an hour writing a letter or by a team of three of four analysts working full-time for some weeks. Usually there is no way to predict how many tasks or what level of effort will be required from a policy shop. It is difficult to forecast the staff resources required for analysis, both in type and quantity, until an issue is presented and the policy climate in which it resides is examined.

Policy shops sometimes need outside help to smooth out the surges of demand for analysis and permit better allocation of limited manpower and resources. The policy staff provides the basic analytical capability for addressing policy issues; general policy-analysis expertise remains in-house. The credibility of a shop breaks down when the staff has contracted out too much of its analysis. In the end, the staff bears the sole responsibility for the analyses it presents to the decision-maker.

To some extent the assessment person has many of the same psychological and career rewards as the scientist, in the sense that he is able to exercise some professional creativity in producing a product. Further, he is personally identified with the output and can use the work to enhance his professional career. These professionals often become internationally recognized experts in various issues or techniques and reap considerable financial and ego satisfaction from their work.

On the other hand, many assessment people and other technical specialists in applied science are seen by the basic scientists as belonging to a stepsister profession. When the research in applied science is formally trained as a scientist and identifies with that community, this prejudice may be personally troublesome. The "retreading" of scientists—moving from basic to applied research—does not help this image problem, as many of those who so transfer are seen as "burned out." Such pejorative descriptions have often resulted in resistance to having groups or universities do research on demand—a potential loss for both the client and the researchers.

Quality

Maintaining objectivity in the course of doing an analysis is a constant problem for policy staff. Normally, civil servants approach their work with a high degree of personal objectivity because they are hired to be impartial with respect to the public they serve. Therefore, in theory, public sector analysts and managers who fund research attempt to be objective in their work, fully expecting that the decision-maker, usually politically appointed, will factor into his decision the necessary political realities. But objectivity in an organization person is often a subjective concept, as Rufus Miles and others have so aptly observed. Miles's Law is "Where you stand depends on where you sit."[21] It is his contention that no person can entirely rise above his institutional perspectives and responsibilities when asked to perform in a statesmanlike fashion. The analyst, research manager, and decision-maker should remain acutely aware of the reality embodied in Miles's Law in going about their work. It is not so certain, however, whether the analytically oriented analyst or the scientifically trained manager would readily admit that he held such a bias, even subconsciously.

Clients

The form and content of a policy analysis are often influenced considerably by the known or anticipated desires and demands of the decision-maker for whom it is being prepared. This may have many manifestations. When the decision-maker perceives himself to be an expert in a particular area, analysts preparing policy papers for him sometimes find that their responsibilities change from merely performing an analysis to participating in a professional contest with the manager over using the "appropriate" assumptions and recognizing the "proper" alternatives. Although such a situation might result in better policy analyses, it might just as easily result in more elegance in their form—which is not commensurate with the importance of the ultimate decision. Elegance is often a luxury ill afforded in the time-pressured policy area.

At the other extreme is the policy-maker who is not familiar with many of the technical aspects of the arena in which the decisions are to be made. In such circumstances, policy papers have to be more detailed and sometimes more tutorial.

Then there is the decision-maker who cares little for analysis and tends to use policy analysts as general staff, even to the point of post hoc justification of preconceived policy decisions. Lastly, there is the decision-maker who has a tendency to let things "suffice," i.e., to want only a level of analysis sufficient to render a decision that is "good enough."[22] This tendency is problematical when the policy under consideration is in the regulatory area: a poor decision (because of poor information) may result in the courts' adjudicating science findings, further confounding the applied-research task.

ATTEMPTS TO WED THE MODELS

In this chapter we have reviewed the psychology, institutions, and motivations of the scientist, other professionals and, for our purposes, the ultimate user of science, the analyst. The public sector employs many from hybrid professions, such as the applied scientist and the assessor, standing somewhere in between the analyst and the scientist—closer to one stereotype or the other, depending on such factors as the issue, institution, and individual. Now we bridge the extremes of scientist and analyst to emphasize the need of smooth transitions from one field to the other.

One of the most vocalized concerns of scientists is that politicians and administrators might dictate analytic agenda or, worse, preordained conclusions, thereby polluting the "pristine waters" of the research community. A guard against such unwarranted intrusion is the science community's peer review system based upon self-regulation. At its extreme this system has an art-for-art's-sake flavor. To some extent our thesis takes issue with the extremes: complete academic license versus bending research results to fit particular policies. In Chapter 2 we decided that self-regulation was appropriate in basic research but not in applied research. The research we are addressing is that which is funded by an agency with a congressional mandate to perform specific governmental functions, usually in a given time period—and this may be either basic or applied research.

To some extent, a constraining of scientific freedom takes place naturally in the normal course of agencies' doing business in the modern research community. Specific research disciplines naturally turn to specific mission agencies on a selective basis. Atmospheric physicists may turn to the National Oceanic and Atmospheric Administration and the Environmental Protection Agency, for example. In fact, even specialities within these major disciplines commonly align themselves with sections of mission agencies, apparently without anyone's feeling his professional rights have been violated. Physicists, chemists, biologists, and those in various subdisciplines, all line up at the appropriate funding units as established by the legislative charter of the agency to do research in a particular area. If the scientific community is willing to accept such direction and constraint as a matter of course, the question becomes, "How much more can still be done without damage to the integrity of the research?" We answer, "A good deal more."

The stereotypes of the scientist and analyst clearly suggest that they approach a problem quite differently. The Babel-like situation that often results when people of different backgrounds are not able to talk to one another suggests that any administrative model concerned with communication should focus more on their need to recognize the professionalism of each other and less on the formal institutional structure that is designed to transfer information between them. The conflict becomes more acute when research units are part of operating agencies that have a clearly understood mandate to perform and need information from the scientific community to do so. In such conditions pressure is created to direct science into areas that may or may not be currently of interest, or "significant," to the scientific community.

But even if the scientist sees the need to play a role in public decision-making, especially as it affects science policy, he does so with some reluctance. The more time spent on policy matters, the less time spent in the labs. Further, it is one thing to be flattered at being asked for advice; it is quite another to get down in the Washington mud and wallow for attention and funds along with the rest of the lobbyists.

To reconcile the pressures of mission agency needs and science community desires, the research managers, for pure survival, must present their budgets in terms that justify their programs in the light of an agency's mission, even if the research actually being done is not completely relevant at that time. This difficulty is most apt to come about for the reason that research projects typically take years to complete and policy imperatives accelerate. Further, the analysts press for data or results before the science community is willing to admit them to its own body of knowledge. This is a clear challenge to the science community, which attempts to address questions or hypotheses in terms of "right" or "wrong"—not in terms of "best guess," which the serious basic scientist regards as irresponsible. On the other hand, the morality of producing and presenting such preliminary results, even in the light of uncertainty, has to be weighed against that of taking a mission agency's funds and not aiding in the fulfillment of that agency's mission.

History is filled with bad decisions which would have been avoided if they could have been postponed a few more years, to allow for further scientific research and testing. In the nineteen-twenties, when the federal government permitted the addition of lead akyls to motor gasoline, further physiological studies would have shown less human tolerance for lead, and a projection of the growth of automobile use might have led to greater caution. Forcing stringent emission controls on cars in the early seventies resulted in huge numbers of poorly performing, fuel-inefficient automobiles on the highways; after a few more years of research and testing the industry was able to produce clean, efficient, reliable, and effectively performing cars. If more information on the effects of asbestos on human beings had been available during the thirties, the federal construction code requirements for asbestos fireproofing might have been altered. More research on food additives would no doubt have precluded the premature approval of certain carcinogenic substances, and might have allowed the use of certain other beneficial substances that were banned on the basis of insufficient research. Further testing would have shown that the drug thalidomide would cause birth defects.

The question is, how long do we wait for the research to be completed? The innately inquisitive nature of the scientist renders him reluctant to issue a final definitive report until every last detail has been thoroughly investigated. Most of our contemporary problems are so complex that such a complete study could take decades or longer. At the same time, increased public awareness and information demand solutions to problems immediately. It is difficult for the politician to say "I don't know—I'll get back to you on that" or "I understand your problem, but I don't have a solution yet." It is more politically palatable to proclaim a quick, simplistic solution, like banning the use of a substance or activity or forcing an industry to do something.

A key responsibility of the policy analyst is to mediate between the purveyance of scientific facts and the demands for political action. There is a need for analysis that recognizes the uncertainty of scientific data and knows how to factor that uncertainty into its recommendations. Today's rapid-fire policy and seemingly endless regulatory calendar and its apparently voracious need for information, often about issues never before addressed, challenge us to streamline the information transfer process in a professional and technically responsible fashion. The procedures discussed later in this work point out some of the ways an accelerated information time line can be addressed effectively. Before we go on to these, however, let us look at how government departments have done this in the past, as examples of formal processes that tried to perform the dissemination function.

The next chapter provides an analysis of several research and development management systems (with emphasis on two, the Environmental Protection Agency's Needs System and the Department of Energy's Environmental Development Plan), that should improve our understanding of how scientific research and the resulting knowledge may be transferred to the public policy and information arenas.

Notes and References

1. Robert K. Merton, "The Normative Structure of Science," *The Sociology of Science*, University of Chicago Press, Chicago, Illinois, 1973, p. 270.

2. International Institute of Applied Systems Analysis, *Annual Report 1977*, Vienna, 1978.

3. International Council of Scientific Unions, *1979 Year Book*, Paris, 1979.

4. Although it is a highly prestigious organization, the National Academy of Sciences is not beyond some rather severe criticism; see Philip M. Boffey, *The Brain Bank of America*, McGraw Hill, New York, 1975.

5. Kuhn calls this body of accepted knowledge a scientific paradigm. Thomas Kuhn, *The Structure of Scientific Revolutions*, University of Chicago Press, Chicago, Illinois, 1962.

6. Price points out that this established curriculum of undergraduate education is one of the common meeting grounds of basic scientists and technologists. As such, it helps the two groups to maintain communications with each other and enables science and technology to develop "in phase." Derek de Solla Price, *Science Since Babylon (Enlarged Edition)*, Yale University Press, New Haven, Connecticut, 1976, pp. 129–130.

7. In the sciences this is called the concept of reliability, defined by Kaplan as "a measure of the extent to which a measurement remains constant as it is repeated under conditions taken to be constant." It is one of the central concepts of science. Abraham Kaplan, *The Conduct of Inquiry*, Chandler, Scranton, Pennsylvania, 1964, p. 200.

8. In an intriguing, though not always convincing, quantitative study of high-energy physicists, Cole and Cole conclude that science advances primarily on the shoulders of a few great men and women and that the cumulative role of the plodders is negligible. Jonathan R. Cole and Stephen Cole, "The Ortega Hypothesis," *Science*, Vol. 178, October 22, 1972, pp. 368–375.

9. This has been demonstrated quantitatively in the biomedical sector.

J. Davidson Frame, "Sixteen Year Trends in Biomedical Funding and Publication," contract report submitted to the Office of Program Analysis, National Institutes of Health, March 15, 1980.

10.   R. A. Muller, "Innovation and Scientific Funding," *Science*, Vol. 209, August 22, 1980, pp. 880–883.

11.   Of course, the new insights brought about by improved instrumentation may force us ultimately to reformulate some of our views of nature. This is dramatically seen in the space sciences, where interplanetary space probes and orbiting observatories are giving us a much clearer view of the world beyond the Earth's atmosphere. See, for example, Dietrick F. Thomsen, "Will Astronomy Go Into Orbit?", *Science News*, Vol. 118, August 30, 1980, pp. 138–140.

12.   The problems that might raise for the scientific community were eloquently discussed by Alvin Weinberg in his seminal article, "Criteria for Scientific Choice," *Minerva*, Vol. 1, Winter 1963, pp. 159–171.

13.   Drucker is severly critical of this process and sees it as contributing to the problems the United States has in maintaining strong university-industry links. Peter Drucker, "Science and Industry, Challenges of Antagonistic Interdependence," *Science*, Vol. 204, May 25, 1979, pp. 808–809.

14.   Robert K. Merton, "The Normative Structure of Science," *The Sociology of Science*, University of Chicago Press, Chicago, Illinois, 1973, p. 270.

15.   Norman W. Storer, "The Internationality of Science and the Nationality of Scientists," *International Social Science Journal*, Vol. 22, 1970, pp. 89–104.

16.   A recent example of this is the case of Elias Alsabti, who has been accused of plagiarizing some sixty scientific papers and of doctoring his curriculum vitae. The accusations of plagiarism have cost Alsabti his job, and it is unlikely that any research institute would now hire him as a researcher. William J. Broad, "Would-Be Academician Pirates Papers," *Science*, Vol. 208, June 27, 1980, pp. 1438–1440.

17.   William F. Sander, "Promoting an Effective R&D/Marketing Interface," *Research Management*, July 1980.

18.   L. J. Peter, *The Peter Principle: Why Things Go Wrong*, Bantam Books, New York, 1970.

19.   W. E. Sauder, *Management Decision Methods for Managers of Engineering and Research*, Von Holt Reinhold Company, New York, 1978, p. 9.

20.   Michael Kiren, "Science vs. Government. A Reconsideration," *Policy Science*, Vol. 12, Elsevier Scientific Publishing Company, Amsterdam, 1980, pp. 333–353.

21.   R. Miles, Jr., "The Origin and Meaning of Miles' Law," *Public Administration Reviews*, No. 38, 1978.

22.   Herbert A. Simon, "Theories of Decision-Making in Economics and Behavioral Science," *American Economic Review*, June 1959, pp. 253–283.

CHAPTER 4

Real-World Experience

The seeming inability to conduct appropriate scientific research routinely, and to transfer the resulting knowledge into the public policy and information arenas effectively and efficiently, is certainly not due to any lack of effort or of management schemes. Most large federal research and development programs have extensive procedures for program direction based on variations of the "management by objectives" concept.[1] None of them, however, has been judged totally successful by the customers (senior federal executives, Congress, public-interest groups). This chapter examines systems used by the Environmental Protection Agency and the Department of Energy and highlights their strong and weak points. These two agencies were chosen for examples of research programs in environment, health, and safety that clearly support a policy or regulatory mission of an agency.

EPA's research has no comprehensive authorizing legislation. Instead it has research authorities under nine separate acts: the Clean Air Act (CAA), the Federal Water Pollution Control Act (FWPCA), the Safe Drinking Water Act (SDWA), the Federal Insecticide, Fungicide, and Rodenticide Act (FIFRA), the Public Health Service Act (PHSA), the Noise Control Act (NCA), the Marine Protection Research and Sanctuaries Act (MPRSA), and the National Environmental Policy Act (NEPA). Most of these laws contain broad, essentially all-encompassing authorizations for research and development on the "control, prevention, abatement, effects" of pollution. Overlapping these broad authorizations are many specific authorizations or even mandates that relate to work on specific problems (acid mine drainage, lake restoration, etc.) or that authorize certain special types of funding for eligible grantee or contractor organizations. Because of the great national interest in energy over the past few years, much of EPA's research relates to the impacts of energy fuel cycles. Similarly, because of strong national environmental interests, the Department of Energy Organization Act of 1977 instructed Assistant Secretaries to advise "the Secretary with respect to the conformance of the Department's activities to environmental protection laws and principles, and [conduct] a comprehensive program of research and development on the environmental effects of energy technologies and programs."

The missions of the research units in the energy area in the two agencies, EPA and DOE, were so similar that both the Congress and the Office of Management and Budget at various times wanted to be assured that the specific programs and projects being undertaken were not directly duplicative. In fact, certain programs were actually transferred between agencies from time to time. Although this close matching in mission caused some budgetary worries, it gives us a rare opportunity to study how two different management groups handle similar research missions. To make this analysis as complete as possible, the EPA organization is followed through three organizational iterations. The DOE organization remained essentially the same throughout the period that EPA went through its changes. Before we look at these agencies, let us briefly look at the experience of other groups.

SELECTED MANAGEMENT EXPERIENCES

We discussed in the opening of Chapter 1 how others handled basic research. Here we shall look at that class of research activity which is directed at particular problems, issues, or regulations. A specific solution is sought, usually in a specified (relatively short) period of time. The variety of organizational and institutional arrangements actually employed by federal agencies to accomplish this goal ranges all the way from in-house research and development laboratories or centers to exclusively extramural research. In the study by Wert et al.[2] the case studies come from the National Institutes of Health, the U.S. Department of Agriculture, the National Aeronautics and Space Administration, the Department of Defense, and the Office of Equal Opportunity. Little is gained here by covering these different organizational arrangements in detail; by looking at their procedures compositely, however, we shall have a useful backdrop for our examples of environment, health, and safety at EPA and DOE. The ten or so programs described had several features in common:

- Because the nature of the work performed by the case study group was usually "on demand" and specific, most of the agencies pulled together ad hoc teams of bureaucrats to manage on a project-by-project basis (for example, by using matrix management mix of subject studied by discipline).

- Program planning is usually in response to specified end points and requirements. Output tends to be specific as is the time frame in which the product is required.

- Projects are selected, often on the basis of very explicit analytical techniques. End results are specified, alternative approaches are delineated and compared with each other, a solution is arrived at, and a choice is made by priority.

- The in-house staff has a great deal of influence over all phases of the research, from generation to selection to monitoring to evaluation.

- There is a conscious effort to utilize the research and development results. The quality of the product and its utility are characteristically not judged by peer group opinion but by the funding organization.

The differences among the specific institutional management techniques are frequently based on the characteristics of either the user community or the parent organization of the research group. For example, the National Institutes of Health groups reported in the study are closer to basic research than others because their parent agency is basic-research-oriented. The most noticeable difference can be found between those groups that perform research in-house and those that contract it out. The rest of the variations in method studied are really slight differences in organizational structure of operation, such as the degree to which in-house staff has control over the phases of the research process.

Looking further at similarities and differences, we begin to see that our generalizations about organizations, practitioners, and goals in the preceding chapters hold up pretty well. The expected product is fairly well understood and specified by the group funding the research. The whole process, then, becomes one dedicated to getting the product in the most efficient manner possible. The manager's task becomes one of first choosing among all of the research projects that might ideally be wanted and then reducing the number to those which he is able to afford. Then from within each of the project areas he can afford he chooses the researchers most likely to deliver the product, on time, and on a given budget. Because he is responsible for the product, he monitors the progress of the research carefully. If he is the final user, he adopts it on receipt; if not, he sets in motion a process whereby it is delivered to the end user. This is a very different paradigm from that of basic research, discussed earlier. Now let us look at EPA and DOE with their mission-oriented research groups in the regulatory area to see how they deal with these issues.

THE NEEDS SYSTEM AT EPA, ROUND ONE

The Program Planning and Reporting System was developed to provide EPA's Office of Research and Development (ORD) with planning input.[3] Fundamental to this system was a rigorous adherence to the concept of "planning by objective." Designed to assist ORD in fulfilling the environmental research requirements of EPA and the nation, it involved a formal process of identifying research needs, defining research objectives, developing detailed plans to accomplish these objectives, establishing priorities, and assigning resources and responsibilities for executing approved plans.

In this system it was the responsibility of each Program Area Manager to identify the environmental objectives relative to his own Program Area and to develop integrated, objective-oriented, and prioritized programs to attain them. These candidate objectives came from numerous sources and in a variety of forms: legislative mandates, executive initiatives, agency goals and strategies. They were of high priority bureaucratically and should have commanded the bulk of supporting research resources. There were, however, numerous other research requirements that had to be considered in structuring an overall program:

- Regional Office and Program Office requirements for specific research output

- Research requirements of state and local regulatory agencies

- Specific research outputs in one Program Area to support an objective in another

- Needs identified by the researchers themselves

A management system for obtaining documented input of EPA's

research and development requirements and their priorities was used. Although no longer operative, the Needs System was at least a systematic method of introducing the requirements of the user community to the research program (i.e., the Program Area Manager). This Needs System was designed to catalyze and systematize the research requirements and had two primary functions:

- To assist the Program Area Manager in defining specific research objectives by providing information on the research, development, and demonstration needs of EPA's operating programs, including the priority associated with each as seen by EPA's key operating officials.

- To document the relationship between EPA's requirements and ORD's program activities such that both final output and interim status information could be tracked and delivered to the specific groups needing the research products.

Environmental Research Need Statements were the formal mechanism for the specification of environmental problems that could not be solved satisfactorily with existing scientific knowledge or technology. Needs could be identified by anyone, but they were actively solicited from EPA's regional personnel, from headquarters personnel in EPA's various Program Offices, and from state and local environmental regulatory programs.

To enter the ORD Program Planning and Reporting System formally, needs had to be reviewed, approved, and ranked in priority by one of several Need Sponsors. These sponsors were the EPA Administrator, Deputy Administrator, Assistant Administrators, and Regional Administrators—senior EPA officials who were most familiar with EPA's policies, programs, and overall priorities. Once "sponsored," the needs were prioritized and forwarded to ORD, where they were reviewed by the appropriate Program Area Manager and were then considered, along with other candidate objectives, for incorporation into ORD's proposed program.

The major components and flow of the ORD Program Planning and Reporting System are presented in Figure 3, and the major elements are discussed below; see also Appendix A.

Media/Categorical Strategies   The ORD maintained a series of research strategy papers on subjects corresponding to EPA's "media/categorical" programs—water, air, pesticides, solid wastes, radiation, toxic substances, and noises—and, in addition, to two areas that overlie these: monitoring and environmental management. These papers

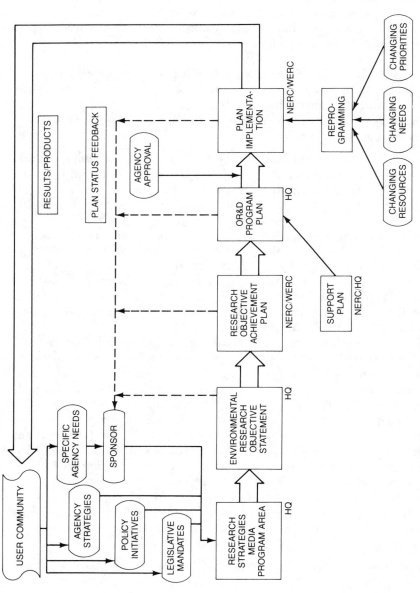

Figure 3. Elements of the Program Planning and Reporting System of the Office of Research and Development. OR&D, Office of Research and Development; NERC, National Environmental Research Center; WERC, Washington Environmental Research Center.

Table 2
The Committees in the Environmental Protection Agency

Program Office	Program Deputy Assistant Administrator's Office	Research Committee, Office of Research and Development	
Office of Air, Noise and Radiation	Office of Radiation Programs	Radiation	Energy Committee
	Office of Mobile Source Air Pollution Control	Mobile Source Air Pollution	
	Office of Air Quality Planning and Standards	Oxidants	
		Gaseous and Inhalable particulate Pollutants	
		Hazardous Air Pollutants	
Office of Water and Waste Management	Office of Water Program Operations	Municipal Waste Water and spill Prevention	
	Office of Water Planning and Standards	Industrial Wastewater	
		Water Quality	
	Office of Drinking Water	Drinking Water	
	Office of Solid Waste	Solid Waste	
Office of Toxic Substances	Office of Testing and Evaluation	Testing and Assessment	
	Office of Program Integration and Information		
	Office of Pesticide Programs	Pesticides	

showed how ORD's research activities flowed logically from the objectives and needs of EPA's regulatory programs, how the various major efforts were interrelated, both programmatically and in timing, and how planned efforts anticipated merging and future problems in environmental protection. With these strategies EPA management was better able to assess the degree to which the research program addressed the environment, both holistically and as made up of discrete media and categorical parts. In addition, the degree to which EPA objectives were realistic in light of the demands they placed on the research program could be better understood. Points of disagreement, such as might occur over the relative priority of any two research objectives, could be put in a clearer perspective when viewed in the context of broad research strategies. Also, the tradeoffs that must be made in initial resource allocation and in midyear reprogramming actions could be better understood.

Program Area Strategies   To summarize the technique, each Program Area Manager was responsible for developing and documenting his strategy for accomplishing the major output and media goals assigned to his specific Program Area. As the manager of a major segment of the ORD activities, he had to be aware of the problems relating to his Program Area that may have required a research, development, and demonstration effort. Environmental Research Objective Statements were prepared, but only for objectives that were of sufficient importance to require a detailed planning effort; so the Program Area Manager was faced with the task of defining the highest-priority research objectives. The Environmental Research Need Statements offered "candidate research objectives" and were considered, with the research strategies, in the preparation of the Environmental Research Objective Statements.

Objectives Statements   The major objectives identified in the Program Area Strategies and the Environmental Research Need Statements were the basis of the Environmental Research Objective Statements. These statements defined specific objectives, with target dates, and provided criteria for evaluating the results and output expected. They constituted directives for developing detailed plans, defined the objectives, and stated when they were required.

Achievement Plans   The Research Objective Achievement Plans defined how objectives would be achieved and identified what resources would be required. They were the basis of all research, development, and demonstration activities conducted by ORD.

Program Plans   The Research Objective Achievement Plans, prioritized by Program Area, plus any additional support plans, provided the input for the generation of the ORD program plan. To develop this plan, the Research Objective Achievement Plans and the Environmental Research Objective Statements were examined, their proposed priority ranking reviewed and modified, and tradeoffs between Program Areas made; the result was a prioritized set of both, within each of ORD's Program Areas. The proposed plan was then forwarded for approval. After approval the designated environmental research centers implemented the tasks necessary to achieve the identified objectives.

The Program Planning and Reporting System had mechanisms for feedback. It was the policy of ORD to conduct its planning in a totally open manner and to afford adequate opportunity for the various operating programs of EPA to participate in the planning process. This allowed for the appeal of any ORD decisions considered unfavorable in light of the documented research requirements and priorities. this interaction was conducted in several ways, beginning with participation in the development of the ORD's research strategy documents. During each annual planning cycle there were also four defined points of direct interface with the operating programs of EPA, two at the policy level and two at the technical level, as follows.

- Interface I, Target-Setting Council: A meeting between EPA's Assistant Administrator for Research and Development and the other Assistant Administrators at the outset of the planning cycle, to receive the counsel of the National Program Managers regarding preliminary resource targets for the various ORD Program Areas.

- Interface II, Needs Refinement: A series of meetings between the planning and technical staffs of ORD and other Program Offices. The primary purpose was to ensure a common understanding of the content of a particular need and its relevance to EPA's strategic goals. With this understanding, truly responsive Environmental Research Objective Statements were to be prepared.

- Interface III, Issue Identification and Research Objective Achievement Plan Refinement: A series of meetings of ORD and Program Office planning and technical staffs following the preparation or revision of detailed plans based on the discussions at Interface II. The purpose was to eliminate "errors of translation" regarding agreements at Interface II and to identify clearly any points of issue between ORD and other Program Offices that might require discussion by senior management.

Interface IV, Issue Resolution: A meeting of all the Assistant Administrators, to resolve, to the extent possible, any remaining issues or to define them sufficiently for presentation to the Administrator or Deputy Administrator for decision.

In addition to the above points of direct planning interaction, the ORD Program Planning and Reporting System incorporated information feedback to the National Program Managers and Regional Administrators (i.e., Need Sponsors) and to Program Area Managers who depended on support activities from other program elements. Decisions relating to objectives, priorities, and timetables were made available to EPA managers, ORD managers, and Need Sponsors on a periodic basis. Such feedback was to assist in ensuring that ORD research activities were responsive to the needs and priorities of EPA and that interrelated programs within ORD were effectively coordinated.

Although the Program Planning and Reporting System in theory was effective, in reality it did not work well. Despite all the enabling Acts' mandates for ORD to "conduct research and development," EPA wanted ORD to support the regulatory functions first and foremost, not to be a research outfit for the good of science. The Needs System, as designed, could have helped to direct the research effort toward work that was seen as useful by the Program Offices. They, however, and the Office of Enforcement, would not take the time to complete the Environmental Research Need Statement forms. Additionally, establishing priorities was difficult because of the following.

- EPA would never explicitly prioritize among the media regulatory programs.

- EPA was continually in a state of organizational flux, and Program Office priorities vacillated widely from month to month.

- Program officials were often noncommittal or uninterested in the formal, research "interface" sessions.

- Research managers, accustomed to projects in at least two-to-five-year time frames, were unable to cope with rapidly changing priorities.

- The research organization had a tendency to try to second-guess the policies of the Program Offices, resulting in bureaucratic warfare rather than communication between the groups.

As a consequence, research priorities often turned out to be a function of the Program Area Managers' personal interests and influence with the EPA Assistant Administrator for Research and Development or the interests of the in-house laboratory doing the work. As a result, the established midyear priorities had little to do with the severity of a problem as perceived by the EPA.

In general the designers of the system felt that they had a successful process in the making. It took a lot of time, though, and a persistent dedication on the part of all the top management team to make it work at all.

ROUND TWO

With the replacement of the first EPA Assistant Administrator for Research and Development, there came a backlash to the formal process set up by the research group. The Needs System was scrapped. In its place, ORD developed a Five-Year Plan to set the research policy in broad, general terms. ORD's mission was seen as being solely in support of EPA's mission-oriented needs, with emphasis on short-to-medium-term research. Basic research was all but eliminated. The program, instead, was to provide the following.[4]

- The scientific and technical base for reasonable standards and regulations

- Standardized methods of measuring and assuring quality control in programs, for assessing environmental quality, implementing regulations, and enforcing standards

- Cost-effective pollution control technology and incentives for acceptance of environmentally sound options

- Scientific, technical, socioeconomic, and institutional methodologies needed for judging environmental management options and balancing them against competing national needs.

The strategy the senior staff at ORD used to develop its Five-Year Plan was based on a series of guidelines:

- Emphasis was given to research designed to protect human health and welfare and natural ecosystems.

- A reasonable balance was to be maintained between responsiveness to immediate technical support and continuing information needs of EPA, and longer-term research to meet future and emerging environmental problems.

- Deliberate attention was to be given to the timely and effective dissemination of technical information and to technology transfer.

- An adequate program of quality assurance was to be maintained.

- Environmental management methods and technology development and demonstration efforts in pollution abatement and environmental restoration were meant to stimulate, assess, and support the development of economically feasible technological solutions, to identify and foster improved management techniques, and to identify and evaluate institutional approaches to implementing technological options.

- Solutions to environmental problems that minimize costs, energy usage, and undesirable transfer of pollutants to other media were to be emphasized.

The total list of guidelines essentially followed the programs already existing in the organizational subunits of ORD, as set up under the previous Administration. In effect, almost any program that ORD's staff wanted to pursue could have been supported under these general guidelines.

The Office of Technology Assessments (OTA) undertook a review of this first Five-Year Plan by using several panels of experts. In the main, it was concerned that there was a failure in the Plan to support long-term basic research. The Plan was repeatedly taken to task for its excessive focus on mission-oriented needs. Regardless of what one might think of the specifics of the Plan, it is ironic that it should have been so criticized; however, given the differences in viewpoint between basic and applied research and the divergence of management styles and objectives that the science perspective generates, and given the fact that the review panels were largely made up of scientists, the criticism is understandable. On the other hand, even though the scientists might object, the Congress should have been expected to be pleased. as the research was targeted to be useful to the regulatory goals it set. To the extent that OTA reflected its will, though, it was not.

The real problem with the Plan, according to OTA, and in fact with the whole management process used by EPA during this period, was its lack of a formal method of setting priorities. The whole planning process was vague and ad hoc. In a summary statement OTA characterized the Plan as follows:

The planning procedure followed by ORD has been character-ized by one observer as a "middle-up middle-down" approach. This process involved soliciting candidate research topics from various headquarters and field offices within EPA, aggregating these tasks into programs within the four ORD project offices, developing a draft 5-year plan around these programs, soliciting comments on this draft throughout the Agency, assigning dollar and staff resources to the various programs, and publishing the final plan.

Because of this haphazard process, the implementation of the Plan led to several unfortunate results:

- The pressure-cooker environment of the media program offices, which set the regulatory standards, resulted in a call for research with immediate answers; long-term research was ignored.

- The plan was developed *in-vacuo* in terms of the total EPA mission and expectations over the ensuing several years.

- No explicit priority-setting system was put in place.

- The mission and its accomplishments were presented as if they were the only institutional arrangement possible for carrying out the research or program of the EPA.

- The effort did not result in identifiable or responsible research programs.

- The Plan was a program based solely on the subjective judgments of the ORD personnel.

These changes in the direction of ORD's research program moved further away from basic research, further away from research that the science community thought relevant (as opposed to what EPA's mission personnel thought relevant), and closer to engineering so-lutions. ORD took note of the OTA critique but continued its course, as set in the first Plan, and the second. It took still another change of Assistant Administrators at EPA to address some of these issues.

ROUND THREE

With the advent of the next Assistant Administrator for Research and Development at EPA, the scientists and research managers in EPA's laboratories found themselves moving further and further away from meaningful decisions about what research to carry out and finally concentrated almost exclusively on how it was to be done.

The next management team to run ORD pictured its mission as akin to that of a research and development shop in a large corporation in the private sector. They saw the same pull and tug for them to emphasize a particular facet of a research project to satisfy the needs of a particular unit, and the same lack of time to meet the requirements that a management team doing similar work in the private sector would experience. They took charge of the organization with a legacy of accusations of its being unresponsive and random in its program planning. The most troublesome area, they felt, was criticism from the other offices within EPA. The scientists had resisted as best they could their loss of research freedom and control over what research would be done and when. The scheme the new team developed moved the research scientists even further toward an "on demand" operation than the second group had.

The management team formed an intraagency task force to determine research needs and management strategy. They found, as a result of the effort, that there was an insensitivity to longer-range research needs, unresponsiveness to the other parts of EPA, and research that was of uneven quality in the existing ORD program. The first and second of these findings, as we said earlier, are potentially mutually exclusive goals. Some care therefore had to be exercised to ensure that they both were considered in an appropriate fashion. The process decided upon was as follows. See also Table 2.

A collegial group of staff members, a committee from both ORD and the Program Office (the client), was formed. This committee sometimes had regional members and others from the headquarters. It developed the Program Plan for its area, set the budget, developed a multiyear plan, and prioritized the projects. It also acted as an ongoing forum for EPA-wide communication on topics of interest and as a place to settle squabbles. Finally, it was the quality control group for the final product. The committee had a given amount of funds to allocate. In this way it became the de facto research manager. This gave the Program Office some control over the research funds without going the whole way and having the funds transferred to it.

It is unclear what the exact role of the ORD personnel should be under such a scheme. In truth, their participation would depend on the personalities of the committee itself. The ORD research managers still had formal responsibility for the funds, however. To some extent, the committees were the ultimate in communication, in that "we" and "they" became as one. To make such a group work, the research staff had to be very explicit about what was to be done and when, and how to set priorities in a reasoned manner. The committees (thirteen in all) controlled over 90 percent of the research budget.

The priorities within Program Areas in response to specific office needs were set by the committees. The prioritization scheme adopted was Zero-Based Budgeting (ZBB), the popular management gimmick of the Carter Administration. As elsewhere, "decision units" (programs) were structured and then ranked by ORD and the Program Offices. The units that survived the ZBB process were made the basis of operating plans for the research laboratories the following year. These plans were more detailed, and they were the contract basis between the laboratories and the research managers at headquarters.

Much effort was expended to ensure that ORD headquarters and laboratories prepared the necessary backup to document each decision unit. The units were then prioritized by ORD managers and the committee chairment. The process then moved on from the committee to the budget review forum of EPA as a whole, with several iterations before arriving at the final budget.

The budget, and its implementation device—the operating plan that is prepared by the ORD laboratory—was subjected to continued review by the committees. In the main, ZBB and the use of research committees was a reasonable way to go about planning a research budget; it makes priorities explicit and involves people at all levels of the management chain. But it replaced decision rules, set by a formal algorithm, with a human system, at the same time more flexible and more time-consuming. It was said by some that the system degenerated into one where little was done by the ORD headquarters staff beyond research and budget planning. Planning had become an end in itself.

The use of committees and consensus management turned out to be a very time-consuming process. The delineation of power and responsibility was not explicit, and so time was spent in turf battles and arguments over process.

Now let us turn to the scheme used at the Department of Energy, which, remember, was pursuing research along similar lines.

THE ENVIRONMENTAL DEVELOPMENT PLAN AT DOE

The Department of Energy's Environmental Development Plan, like the Needs System of EPA, was created to coordinate the research of disparate units, integrate the environmental research requirements of researchers and users, and ensure that the results from one part of the program would be available when needed by another.

In the following pages this process will be examined in great detail—possibly greater than the average reader will deem necessary. The reason for such detail, however, is to present the process with enough information to be of use to someone who might want to design a similar system and, more importantly, to convince the reader that the formal mechanism was a serious effort on the part of DOE to design a transfer procedure.

The Environmental Development Plans (EDP) were first conceived and implemented in the Energy Research and Development Administration (ERDA) before it was absorbed into DOE. To institutionalize this process in ERDA, a formal order was developed and signed on December 14, 1976. A general policy statement of this order said:[5]

> ERDA is committed to protection and enhancement of environmental quality, through development of environmentally acceptable energy systems. To this end, ERDA recognizes its responsibility in the environmental area as one of impact identification, characterization, analysis, assessment and solution development for all energy systems and translation of this information into environmental issues for use in decisionmaking at the earliest stages.

To this end, the directive defined an EDP as "the basic document for planning, budgeting, managing, and reviewing the environmental activities for each energy system." The EDP was designed to (1) identify environmental issues (including occupational and public health and safety, socioeconomic, ecological, cultural, and aesthetic issues), (2) include an assessment of the current stage of knowledge related to environmental problems and identification of major topics requiring research, development, and demonstration, (3) outline research, development, and demonstration strategies directed at further identification and resolution of environmental problems, (4) designate significant milestones, and (5) estimate resource requirements.

Thus the EDP was supposed to be a way of identifying environmental issues and scheduling appropriate research and analysis for each energy system. As separate documents, the EDP's are tailored to the unique characteristics of both technology and environmental programs. In combination with the relevant program plan, an EDP-guided research to ensure that the energy system was environmentally acceptable. The intent of this process was to facilitate the transfer of scientific research to the assessment community.

The process required coordination with several offices and ongoing activities within DOE and concurrence with several people before being submitted to the Assistant Administrator for the Program Offices (in ERDA) and to the Assistant Administrator for Environment and Safety, for final approval. See Figure 4.

The proposed design of the EDP itself was fairly complex. Figure

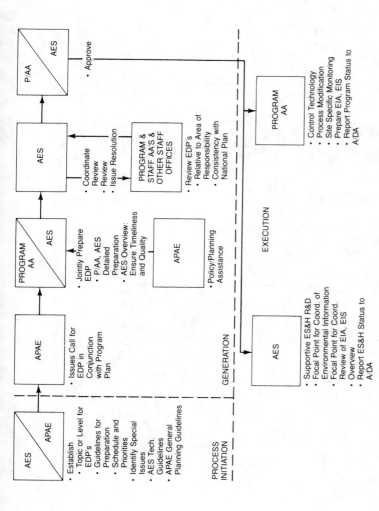

Figure 4. Flowchart of the Environmental Development Plan (EDP) of the Energy Research and Development Administration. AA, Assistant Administrator; A/DA, Administrator or Deputy Administrator; AES, Assistant Administrator of Environment and Safety; APAE, Assistant Administrator of Policy Analysis & Evaluation; EIA, Environmental Impact Assessment; EIS, Environmental Impact Statement; ES&H, environment, safety, and health; P/AA, (cognizant) program assistant administrator, R&D, research and development.

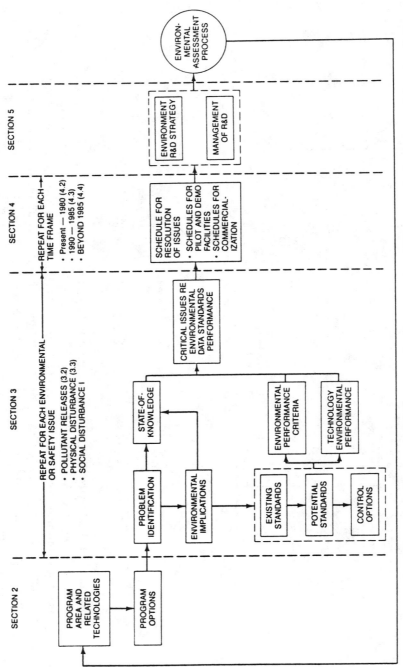

Figure 5. Organization of the Environmental Development Plan (EDP) document suggested by the Energy Research and Development Administration.

5 indicates the very detailed information to accompany the total development and deployment of each technology throughout the time frame covered in ERDA's energy plan (to the year 2000); obviously, it is an ambitious undertaking both substantively and administratively. The first generation of EDP's, completed in FY 1977, was prototypical and consisted of 26 documents for selected fossil, nuclear, solar, geothermal, and advanced energy systems, and conservation programs.

Of the sections that follow, those on the first-generation EDP's and the Program and Project Management System are taken from the House and Monti paper on DOE's environmental planning process.

First-Generation Plan

It is not surprising that the EDP's, being first-of-a-kind efforts to link environmental considerations with technology evolution in a systematic way, should draw both praise and criticism. Even in preparation, the scope and ultimate contents of the documents were influenced by the varying perceptions the preparers had of the EDP's purpose. An EDP could be perceived as an issue definition document, a research definition document, an environmental "forcing" mechanism, or a straight program implementation plan. Commentators on the first-generation results tend to be biased by these conflicting perceptions, individual preconceptions, or problems in using the information.

One of the first activities undertaken by the new Office of Environment, in DOE, was to review the EDP's to determine how well they met the needs of DOE's new missions.[6]

The mission of DOE, with its more pragmatic approach to managing research and development in support of short-term and near-term energy policy, placed increased stress on the timeliness and adequacy of environmental information at decision points in the development cycle. Failure to anticipate environmental information needs and to mount the required research program would directly affect the time line for technology development and its availability for policy execution.

The review of the first-generation EDP's indicated that they were excellent general statements for defining the technologies' potential environment, health, and safety impacts. They correlated generalized environment, health, and safety research needs with the existing program, and their relatively consistent format facilitated comparison of these factors and research and development requirements across technologies. The EDP's were descriptive rather than analytic documents and hence did not directly provide the information or analysis required for establishing program priorities or environmental performance criteria. The intended purpose, of providing an important basis for planning and conducting environmental activities by the many organizations involved in research, development, and demonstration, was accomplished. See Appendix B.

Specific problem areas were identified in the review:

Format

- The similar report formats, while aiding in EDP cross-comparisons, may have restricted the identification of differences particular to the stages of technology development.

- In their original form the EDP's would have limited value in disseminating comprehensive environment, health, and safety information (all of the DOE energy programs) to diverse audiences.

Content

- The level of detail varied greatly among EDP's and inhibited cross-comparisons.

- Emission factors relative to current or proposed standards should have received greater emphasis. Ambient effects, which may be a function of several technologies, were overemphasized.

- Socioeconomic and critical resource impacts were sometimes not adequately addressed.

- The link between technology and environment, health, and safety research and development schedules was sometimes not apparent, or further analysis was needed to ensure this linkage.

- Technology descriptions were sometimes overemphasized.

Responsibilities

- The EDP frequently contained no clear delineation of implementation responsibilities among divisions and offices.

The General Accounting Office also had something to say about the success of this initial coordination process:[7]

> The ERDA Office of Environment and Safety focused its environmental efforts on nuclear and fossil energy technologies. Officials within this office had extensive previous interactions with ERDA officials involved in nuclear energy RD&D and, accordingly, had been able to closely coordinate and integrate its environmental R&D efforts into nuclear energy technology

development activities. However, this office had not been successful in developing a similar close relationship with officials involved in fossil energy development and had encountered problems in coordinating and integrating its environmental efforts into fossil energy technologies. As a result, ERDA's efforts to identify, schedule, and carry out needed environmental R&D tasks had been impaired.

Although the report documents in several pages the difficulties between the Office of Environment and Safety and some portions of the fossil energy research program, it does give support to the idea of EDP's and suggests that DOE do its best to ensure that the difficulties experienced between offices be overcome:[7]

> We recommend that you closely monitor the (1) conduct of the environmental R&D program, giving particular attention to coordination and cooperation problems, and (2) development and implementation of DOE's Policy and Program Planning System, including the procedures for integrating and using Environmental Development Plans, to ensure the timely and effective integration of environmental and energy technology development activities.

The Plan in the DOE

The opportunity for further EDP development and modification came about with the formation of DOE and the creation of the Office of Environment. DOE also issued a directive on the need for an EDP.[8] This order simplified the procedure somewhat, so that only the Assistant Secretary for Environment and the Assistant Secretary for the subject technology program were responsible for the documents, and the Assistant Secretary for Policy and Evaluation was responsible for integrating the EDP into the planning process of DOE.

The major objective of the EDP system was to provide environmental information at the time an energy program decision was in review. It assumed the establishment of relative priorities for DOE energy programs based principally on information from the energy program office and the Assistant Secretary for Policy and Evaluation. A major difference between the first and the second generation of EDP's was that environmental analyses associated with energy program decision points would be scheduled and summarized in the EDP's. This information promoted the inclusion of environmental considerations, as well as of technical and economic factors, in decision-making.

In general, measures were taken to improve the system:

- By focusing more explicitly on the significant issues inherent in the technology at each stage in its development.

- By introducing a more formal procedure for analysis, to assess the results of ongoing research and provide a direct information input to the decision process (an Environmental Readiness Assessment, see below).

The identification of the significant environmental concerns continued to be the heart of the EDP. Fundamentally, two generic questions guided this identification process:

- Do standards or regulations for a source emission or effluent exist, and is the technology, in its current state, capable of meeting them?

- Does sufficient information exist to make an authoritative judgment that the technology can be installed and operated with reasonable or acceptable risk to the environment?

The judgment of experts was sought to confirm the answer to these questions. The judgments were to be derived largely from empirical evidence at hand and from assessments of the probable impacts of the technology for assumed sets of conditions.

The EDP scheduled, in conjunction with the identification of the nodes in the decision network, the preparation of Environmental Readiness Assessments, which were the mechanism for decision on the acceptability of technologies at the decision nodes. The results of the assessment were published in an Environmental Readiness Document.

These measures were applied to a second generation of EDP's, 34 documents that were published in 1979 and 1980; see Appendix C.

A Mid-Course Correction

Within DOE the whole planning process evolved at the same time the second generation of EDP's was being formed. A strong central planning office similar to that in ERDA did not develop. Instead, a program planning system based on technology program and project plans was instituted by the DOE Under Secretary. An internal memo on the relationship of EDP's to the planning process of DOE gives perspective on this development:[9]

As I am sure you are aware, strong consideration is currently being given to the idea of abandoning a formal centralized planning structure in favor of a loosely knit collection of whatever plans the Assistant Secretaries develop on their own. This approach evolves from the feeling that the obvious lack of secretarial support for centralized planning and the dismal history of planning systems generally, do not create an atmosphere conducive to effective implementation of a PPPS [Policy and Program Planning System]. While we agree that there has been a demonstrated lack of high level support and that past efforts have not been particularly successful, we see these as isolated problems or failures, not as an indictment of the formal planning concept itself. More importantly from our perspective, however, is the impact of the informal approach on the EDP system.

It is obvious (and somewhat inevitable) that given the exigencies of DOE program management, attention to environmental matters is not high priority for a program manager. Despite the known costs of short-sightedness in government programs, it is an uphill fight for EV [Environment] and Policy (and anyone else who attempts it) to convince the technology programs that the associated environmental research is an imperative part of any development program. Environmental Development Plans, however, have taken significant steps in this direction. By working together to achieve a consensus both program managers and the research community have been better sensitized as to the environmental requirements of each technology. What is lacking at the moment is a forcing mechanism to insure fulfillment of these requirements. A linking of EDP requirements to the plans and commitments in a PPPS would be one useful answer to this problem. It would put environmental research milestones on par with those of the technology and would include them in any high level program reviews/evaluations. If, on the other hand, a loose network of plans is substituted for a PPPS, it is unlikely that EDP's will ever evolve beyond their present state of accomplishment. The present set of EDP's are good first steps, but without further development they are inadequate for the long run. Ultimately, the programs and the department will suffer.

The Program and Project Management System

Despite the reservations in the memorandum cited, a useful forcing mechanism developed with the advent of the DOE Under Secretary's "Program and Project Management System (PPMS) for DOE Outlay Programs."[10] In this system each line manager developed plans for outlay (funded) programs for which the manager was responsible. This planning and documentation effort served a number of important objectives:

• Ensure that all major programs are developed with clear operational, time-phased objectives (multiyear to relate to current budget processes).

- Ensure that all significant projects and activities have clear subobjectives that relate to program objectives.

- Relate program and project and activity objectives to the National Energy Act, National Energy Plan, and related plans and legislation, where possible.

- Provide for determining priorities among programs and projects and, in turn, relate these to various levels of resource availability.

- Avoid commitment of major resources prior to adequate project definition.

- Provide key program and project managers with a clear view of related program and project objectives and plans.

- Provide visibility on all key decisions and timely feedback for all levels of management.

- Maintain accountability through all levels of the organization with a minimal amount of procedure and paperwork.

The basic system elements of special interest to this discussion were the Program Plans, which were the baseline for overall program effort, the Energy System Acquisition Project Plans (ESAPP), which provided a more explicit work breakdown for individual projects within the program, and the Energy System Acquisition Advisory Board (ESAAB), which advised the Under Secretary on key decisions in the development cycle. See Appendix D.

The system concept provided a full opportunity for the EDP to perform its intended function: the environmental complement of a technology program plan. Therefore, in the absence of formal plans for technical programs, the EDP had existed as a separate entity that attempted to match environmental needs with an understood technology program plan. With firmer technology program documentation and approval, the preparation and revision of EDP's were facilitated. Likewise, once firmly coupled with technical programs, the EDP served as a primary resource document for project-level environmental planning.

For an appropriate matching of the EDP to the technology program plans, certain elements of the EDP had to be consistently treated and emphasized or added where they did not exist. One across-the-board adjustment would ensure that all EDP's contained a definite assignment of responsibility for acting on environmental requirements identified in the documents. Another adjustment involved incorporating the estimated resources requirements to accomplish the environmental plan. A third adjustment required a better developed implementation strategy to indicate how the effort and resources were distributed among the projects making up the program.

These later improvements were introduced in the third generation of EDP's. The first example of the complete concept was a new EDP for a DOE program concerned with the diesel engine. Late in FY 1978, by direction of the Under Secretary, DOE undertook development of a light-duty diesel-engine research program whose ultimate goal was to assess the environmental acceptability of the engine. A program plan outlining a research effort and funding plan was prepared, involving the coordinated efforts of three elements of DOE: health effects studies (Environment), diesel-engine-testing (Conservation), and combustion research (Energy Technology). The EDP for this program cited the special environmental concerns associated with diesel exhaust emissions, summarized the current state of knowledge respecting these concerns, developed a general strategy for implementing the environmental research and development, and set forth the integrated schedule for its conduct.

As before, the preparation of EDP's was the joint responsibility of a technical program office and the Office of Environment. The actual work of coordination and preparation was conducted by subcommittees assigned to specific technology programs under the aegis of the Environmental Coordinating Committees (see below).

To implement a process to make the EDP compatible with the Program and Project Management System, a memo was sent to all Assistant Secretaries on December 18, 1978, to make the procedure formal:[11]

> In the program planning concept you have initiated through the PPMS [Program Project and Management System], the EDP should become the environmental complement to the technical component of the plan. Today we have thirty-two (32) EDPs in a state of revision. These address energy technology areas listed in the attachment. These areas need to be aligned to accord with the program areas defined by our office as requiring program plans. Further upgrade of the EDPs will be necessary if they are to serve their intended purpose as a description of an environmental program. In its final format, the EDP would be comprised of six main sections.
>
> 1.   An assessment of concerns and risks relevant to the technology and their status.
> 2.   An identification of concerns not yet satisfactorily resolved or addressed.

3.   A delineation of needed R&D to resolve remaining concerns.

4.   A general implementation strategy.

5.   Integrated milestone schedules including those for meeting NEPA [National Environmental Policy Act] requirements.

6.   Assignment of performing office responsibilities and programmed resources.

In current editions of the EDPs, section 2, 3, and 5 are in a mature state of development; the other sections need to be further developed. The EDPs thus developed will govern the content of Environmental Annexes [renamed Project Environmental Plans; see next section] prepared in consequence of your designation of an Energy System Acquisition Project.

The Project Environmental Plans

DOE prepared, with the cooperation of the technical program offices, a first-generation version of sixty or more Energy System Acquisition Project Environmental Plans (PEP). To the extent practical, material was incorporated from available EDP drafts or was newly developed to meet the spirit and intent of the Program and Project Management System directive. Ultimately, a PEP contained elements of an EDP (program-level plan), but the requirements in it were tailored to the system selected for development and the needs in the ensuing development stages; see Figure 6.

In accordance with a directive from the Under Secretary, the PEP's were updated at decision points in preparation for meetings of the Energy System Acquisition Advisory Board. The EDP was also updated in anticipation of the decision and provided information for preparation of the PEP. This was quite consistent with the view that EDP updates should be rescheduled from an annual cycle to an intermittent cycle matching the needs of the decision process.

Environmental planning, whether at the program or the project level, was based on the most current assessments and evaluation of the environmental status of a technology. To serve this function, the Assistant Secretary for Environment instituted the mechanism of the Environmental Readiness Document noted above, which is described next.

Environmental Readiness Document

The focus of the Environmental Readiness Document (ERD) was the environmental readiness of the technology at a given time for further development or commercialization. In FY 1979. ERD's were prepared, to assist in screening candidates for near-term commercialization.

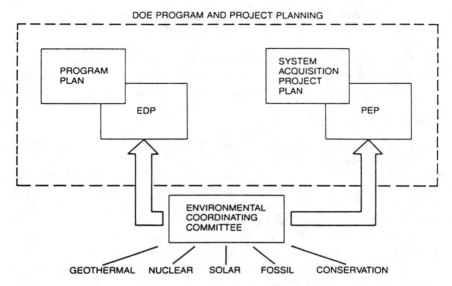

Figure 6. Environmental planning and review system of the Department of Energy (DOE). EDP, Environmental Development Plan; PEP, Energy System Acquisition Project Environmental Plans.

ERD assessment was a critical review of the data and information generated in research and development programs carried on by DOE and others. It did several things:

• As an assessment prepared independently by the Office of Environment, it enabled the Assistant Secretary for Environment to advise and concur on decisions being considered by the Energy System Acquisition Advisory Board.

• It provided the research and development managers with an evaluation of environmental risk and uncertainty in possible applications of the technology, and with an assessment of environmental control technology needs and costs.

• It reviewed the significance of remaining unresolved environmental concerns and directed attention to areas needing priority emphasis in continuing environmental research.

• It supported Environmental Impact Statement preparation. As an analytical reference document, it was useful in outlining environmental concerns and supplying quantitative information on source terms and potential ambient impacts.

ERD's were prepared in consultation with the technical program offices and are reviewed by them and by others having specialized knowledge and interest in the technology.

Utility of Planning Documents

Environmental Development Plans (EDP), Environmental Readiness Documents (ERD), and Project Environmental Plans (PEP) provided DOE with a logical and systematic approach to identifying the environment, health, and safety concerns. These documents became important planning tools for calling out the research and development necessary to address and alleviate those concerns. The process brought DOE's technical and environmental managers together and resulted in a better understanding and airing of environmental matters. It was the mechanism for addressing environmental matters concurrent with technology development. The documents also were used by other agencies and for dealing with the public on environmental matters. See Appendix E.

Environmental Coordinating Committees

To facilitate the communication and interactions so vitally necessary to those three elements (the EDP, ERD, and PEP), Environmental Coordinating Committees were established. The functions of the committees were to provide a forum for the exchange of viewpoints and requirements directed at the preparation of EDP's, ESAPP's (Energy System Acquisition Project Plans), and PEP's, and to oversee their completion and implementation. Experience dictated the following format; see also Figure 7.

- One such committee was confirmed for each of the major technology program areas: nuclear, fossil, solar, geothermal, and conservation. Each had senior program managers from the cognizant program offices and the Office of Environment. The committee was chaired by the Office of Environment and the Office of Technology Impacts.

- Each committee became a two-tier committee. The parent committee was made up of the senior program managers, who were delegated responsibility for the actual preparation of the EDP and ESAPP annex to subcommittees. Each subcommittee identified with an energy system selected from development or com-

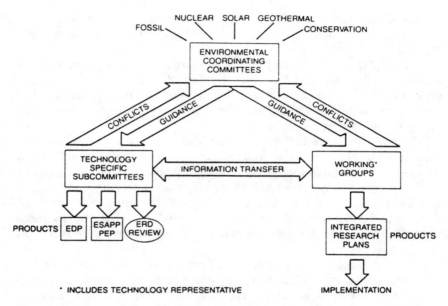

Figure 7. Environmental Coordinating Committees. EDP, Environmental Development Plan; ESAPP, Energy System Acquisition Project Plans; PEP, Energy System Acquisition Project Environmental Plans; ERD, Environmental Readiness Document.

mercialization; for exmaple, under the Fossil Energy Committee a typical subcommittee was Coal Gasification. Subcommittees were made up of project managers and staff engaged in planning. The Office of Environment or the Office of Technology Impacts would chair the subcommittee.

• The parent committee (e.g., Fossil Energy) met only irregularly and infrequently, to resolve conflicts and issues not remedied at subcommittee level.

• Adjunct working groups translated the research needs defined in the EDP and the ESAPP annexes into detailed task plans for implementation at field sites and research laboratories.

Those who participated in working groups were a primary source of needed information for EDP and ESAPP annex preparation and as a general rule sat on the subcommittee as well. Conflicts between programs or significant issues that arose in the field would be reported to the Environmental Coordinating Committee for early resolution.[12]

The ERD's, EDP's, and PEP's were internal management and assessment mechanisms that enabled the DOE to carry out responsibilities imposed by the National Environmental Policy Act of 1969 and the national policy it embodies, while developing energy technologies responsive to national needs.

That Act required all federal agencies to give "appropriate consideration to the environmental effects of proposed actions" in all phases of agency decision-making and to prepare detailed Environmental Impact Statements for all major federal actions significantly affecting the human environment. ERD's, EDP's, and PEP's were all part of the process by which the DOE made sure that energy technologies developed by the agency were environmentally sound and acceptable.

The environmental planning and review process outlined above, with the cooperative efforts of the Office of Environment and technical program staff, ensured that management and control of environmental problems were based on sound knowledge and understanding of technical development and cost-control factors and also that environmental concerns were assessed and integrated into all states of DOE research and development and decision-making.

The formal procedures for linking environmental and technological research continue to evolve through time. The linking of the research of the Office of Environment with that of the technology program offices, neither of which has direct control of, or responsibility for, the research program of the other, represents a problem facing all organizations, public and private, where the research unit is expected to make its work relevant to the mainstream. In large bureaucracies, where changes in policy are usually accomplished by changes in management style, such links are even more difficult. The EDP process was an extremely ambitious undertaking and was among the few successes in establishing such a link.

In summary, the EDP fulfilled its original aim—to provide for planning purposes a formal link across the offices of Assistant Secretaries.

A Strategic Plan

One of the weaknesses of a technology-based process such as the EDP is that it doesn't look across the entire research program, but merely relates research needs to an individual technology and its environmental issues. The development of a Strategic Plan overcame this weakness.[13] The first step was to develop a methodology.

The lack of resources for addressing all research requirements and the responsibility for expending funds judiciously necessitate that research topics and projects be ranked according to "importance" and that resources be allocated according to the ranking. There are no simple, universally accepted procedures for accomplishing either task. The many factors determining importance are usually recognizable, but their relative contributions are matters of judgment. Many theoretical methods of allocating research funds efficiently have been developed, but enough information to apply them without considerable judgment is never available.

For example, a budget might be allocated solely on the basis of the desires of political and other interest groups. Such a strategy might engender the minimum of short-term criticism of the expenditures, because each project could be linked to a specific sponsor or client. On the other hand, it would be difficult to design an integrated program addressing the real issues in this fashion. Further, interest groups come and go, and there is the risk that, in the next budget cycle, the expenditure patterns would not be in agreement with the new interests.

Similarly, only the research seen as necessary by the scientific community might be funded. This method would build a strong support base in the scientific community, but an integrated program focus would tend to suffer. The long-term interests of the scientific community may not correspond to the mission of an operating federal agency. The mismatch would be exaggerated if the research budget were crosscut with other agencies and not directly tied to the sponsoring agency's mission. A case in point is an environmental research budget in an energy agency: because the Assistant Secretary for Environment in the DOE was charged with helping to ensure the development of energy programs in an environmentally acceptable fashion, it had to balance both energy and environmental perspectives.

Because the interest of the Assistant Secretary is in ensuring the environmental acceptability of energy technologies and policies, a research strategy that maximizes information for energy is the optimal one. In such a strategy the issues related to each energy technology or policy are characterized and then ranked in importance; a scoring mechanism is used for ranking across technologies. Research is then planned to address these ranked issues. Because the technique, by design, ranks the most important issues across all technologies, it approaches an efficient allocation of resources from an environmental perspective. This technique is detailed to a greater extent in Appendix F.

SUMMARY AND ASSESSMENT

In summary, there are two basic features to both the EPA and the DOE schemes and their evaluations. The first requirement is that a form of communication be set up between those who manage or do the research and those who use the results for policy purposes. It is highly unlikely that one group would support both functions. Our experience has shown that in these two groups the people, training, operations, and goals of the members are apt to be very different. Therefore, one task is to make sure that the work being done by the research community is indeed that which is likely to be needed by those who do policy or regulatory analysis. Any form of standardized information system which forces the communication and makes one group responsive to the other is acceptable; but someone to whom both groups report is going to have to take responsibility for ensuring that the science group doesn't begin telling the analysts what the emerging policy issues are going to be; at the same time, because science takes time the researchers are going to have to be somewhat insulated from the policy pressure cooker, as policy analysts have a tendency to try to shape the science program to respond to fire-drill orders.

As a way of ensuring against such heavy-handed direction, formal methods are needed to help set priorities in research. They can be fairly standard budgetary schemes (PPBS, MBO, ZBB, or some other spoonful of alphabet soup). The real test of effectiveness is whether they are transparent enough for the users really to understand what they are buying for the research dollar. As long as everyone is using the same system, in the same way, the relative value of research vis-à-vis other expenditures of the tax dollar and the relative value of the rest of the research can be known and understood.

To reiterate, first there must be a formal mechanism to communicate policy needs to the researcher, and then there must be a way to set priorities among needs for the scarce research dollars. The formal systems for doing this are almost immaterial.

As we have seen in our discussion of the EPA and DOE systems, there were certainly attempts on the part of the research managers in these agencies to bridge the gap between science and assessment. The EPA Needs System attempted to survey the various parts of the agency and its regional offices, to ascertain what scientific questions they thought had to be addressed. In the actual implementation of this system several weaknesses appeared.

Concerns articulated by the user community were often in terms not normally used in the science sector. For example, the current interest in doing something about acid rain might translate into a relatively complex research program in the scientific areas of transport, effects, monitoring, epidemiology, and the like. Not only is there wanted a process for translating the needs of the user community into the disciplines of the scientific community, there is also needed a feedback to the user community regarding the extent to which their concerns have been addressed. This two-way communication is generally lacking in the research management systems.

In EPA the translation is done largely by the career bureaucrats, who act as the go-betweens for the scientific laboratories and the program offices. To the extent that the research planned is responsive to EPA's requirements, there is a clear need for those career professionals both to interpret EPA's needs to the scientific community at the laboratory during the time the research program is set in place and to act as a communications link and ensure that the research results are put in a form usable to the program offices.

In DOE no such mechanism exists. The bureaucrats have seen themselves as identified with the science community and do not see the job of translator as part of their mission. In a DOE task force report on health effects assessment they found:[14]

> A health effects assessment function should be established . . . to produce reports on what is known, unknown and uncertain regarding potential human health impacts of principal ongoing DOE programs and major policy issues, and to coordinate the use of health effects assessments with . . . policy, program and NEPA [National Environmental Policy Act] staffs as well as other assessment groups.

The rationale for this group was to gather up the science research and put it in a usable form for the technology offices.

The EPA system, in operation, did not conform to its own guidelines and was viewed by many as a mechanism for justifying what the researchers wanted to do. This criticism pretty well remained under all forms of organizational arrangements but was reduced as the program offices became more involved. Because no organization ever has enough resources, either in money or personnel, the budget allocation process is bound to result in winners and losers. This is institutionally difficult enough for any group, as it disappoints some researchers, who see their programs as clearly the most important of all. Shifting resources affects individual scientists' lives and professions, often in a profound way, and their difficulties are exacerbated when the research is supposed to be responsive to a user community that is diverse in its needs. If it is postulated that a system exists to respond to the diverse needs of a community, the inevitable result of such a system is that some users will not get the information they want, others will not get all they want, and still others will not get their information when they want it. Although the users are likely to be able to understand intellectually that there will not be sufficient resources to serve everyone at the level required, there is apt to be a noticeable lack of magnanimity among individual users who are being asked to subjugate their requirements and admit that their needs are less important than any others. This situation is made worse when the information requested by the user is in response to a congressional mandate—say, to regulate or perform—and the science input is critical to this response. Similar situations exist when programs are on a time line to produce a physical product, and the research on health and safety critical to the production schedule is out of phase.

EPA responded to these difficulties in an apparently rigorous fashion by effectively dividing the research budget into portions that would be dedicated to the needs of specific user groups. The user groups, chaired by the program Assistant Administrators, have fundamental control over this portion of the research and development budget, the excess needs being adjudicated by a group of decisionmakers, in committee fashion. The Assistant Administrator for Research and Development has retained sole control only over the office's basic-research program. It appears that this system would work against those research programs that address several issues of several different users in a scientific fashion and could result in considerable duplication of work in an effort to satisfy the nonscientific user.

The EDP effort of the DOE, in concept, was very similar to EPA's scheme. In general, the process was a formal attempt to get the environmental scientists and the technology users to agree on what research is needed, in what form, and when. The process was designed to identify "issues" that needed to be addressed to ensure that the energy technology would be produced and operated in an environmentally acceptable fashion. In theory, these issues or needs were used to plan both the Office of Environment programs and the technology environmental programs in DOE. There was no formal procedure in place to ensure such compliance, however. For example, the EDP's were not regarded as formal commitments of the cosigners to spend any amount of money during any time period. Even PEP's were subject to the same deficiency. Part of the reason was that there were clearly not enough resources available to fund all the technology issues or needs to the level required.

On the other hand, the Strategic Plan of the Office of Environment did give that office the first look at how well it was doing in addressing the needs of the DOE. The technology and environmental issues, when transferred to the scientific disciplines, resulted in several research projects that are able to address a number of issues specifically by individual technologies. For example, several technologies identified the difficulties due to the thermal pollution of water, associated with power production and use. The effects program in the ecology sector of the scientific community does not really care whether the thermal effects from a fossil, solar, or nuclear plant; the results are equally interesting to each technology.

The results of the Strategic Plan may have been accidental and perhaps cannot be repeated; only further analysis will tell. More fundamentally, it is certain that these results, even if accurate, are not clearly perceived by the scientific or technology sectors. The planning in the Office of Environment was not usually seen as addressing these issues systematically, and the Plan analysis may have been accidental or may have reflected an intuitive response of experienced research managers who know that research efforts are needed. If the latter, the requests of the user community were transformed by the manager into scientific considerations by a weighting scheme. It is hard to present this experience in an empirical fashion that can be reviewed by the users.

Further, there still has to be an educational effort made by the user community to translate its needs into the issues already identified in the EDP's, so that the environmental research program can address these issues. This is to mitigate against the tendency to see the Office of Environment's effort in terms of funds spent rather than issues addressed. To the extent that this is not done, environmental research and development in DOE may follow the EPA by losing control of its research funds.

Both these attempts, along with our observation in the earlier chapters, are sufficient to forge an institutional arrangement for transferring and prioritizing research efforts and results that can be made more effective by incorporating sociopsychological factors that recognize the dynamics of how professionals interact. This is the focus of the next chapter.

NOTES AND REFERENCES

1.   The concept of "management by objectives" is so widely accepted today that detailed descriptions of it can be found in almost every current

text on principles of management; see, for example, Harold Koontz and Cyril O'Donnell, *Essentials of Management* (2nd ed.), McGraw Hill, New York, 1978, Ch. 3.

2. J. Wert, A. Lieberman, and R. Levian, *R&D Management. Methods Used by Federal Agencies*, Lexington Books, D.C. Heath and Company, Lexington, Massachusetts, 1975.

3. U.S. Environmental Protection Agency, Office of Research and Development, "Program Planning and Reporting Manual," Washington, D.C., January 1974, pp. 1–17.

4. U.S. Environmental Protection Agency, Office of Research and Development, *U.S. Environmental Protection Agency Environmental Research Outlook, FY 1976 Thru 1980. Report to Congress,* ORD, EPA-600/9-76-003, 1976.

5. U.S. Energy Research and Development Administration, "Requirement for an Environmental Development Plan (EDP)," ERDA Immediate Action Directive No. 1500.4, December 14, 1976, pp. 1 and 2.

6. U.S. Department of Energy, "Review of the EDP Program," staff paper, Office of Technology Impacts, Office of Environment, January 3, 1978.

7. U.S. General Accounting Office, "Opportunities to Fully Integrate Environmental Research and Development into Developing Energy Technologies," EMD-78-43, April 6, 1978.

8. U.S. Department of Energy, "Environmental Development Plans," Order 5420.1, August 10, 1978 (supersedes Interim Management Directive No. 5102, January 15, 1978).

9. U.S. Department of Energy, "EDP's and PPPS," Memorandum from T. Snyder to J. Janis, August 10, 1978.

10. U.S. Department of Energy, "Program and Project Management System for DOE Outlay Program," Interim Policy and Guidance, May 31, 1978.

11. U.S. Department of Energy, "Environmental Planning and Review in Relation to Major Systems Acquisition Projects," Memorandum from the Assistant Secretary for Environment to Assistant Secretaries for Resource Applications, Energy Technology, and Conservation and Solar Applications, Department of Energy, December 18, 1978.

12. Peter W. House and Dario R. Monti, *Using Futures Forecasting in the Planning Process*, U.S. Department of Energy, Office of Assistant Secretary for Environment, Office of Technology Impacts, April 1979, Appendix C.

13. U.S. Department of Energy, *Strategic Plan*, Office of Environment, Draft, March 1980, pp. 27–30.

14. MITRE Corporation, "Task Force Report on Health Effects Assessment," prepared for the Acting Assistant Secretary for Environment, U.S. Department of Energy, August 1978.

CHAPTER 5

Next Steps

Our search for improvements in information transfer for the policy analysis process has led us into an examination of the applied-research activity itself. Since a large amount of federal research is managed in a demand-oriented atmosphere, several different systems were available for inspection and evaluation. An interdisciplinary analysis of the malfunctions of selected operational systems turned up many correctable situations. These problem areas, however, are not like those found in conventional management science, operations research, or research management. They don't involve defining objective functions, developing management models, assigning priorities, allocating resources, project management systems, information monitoring systems, and the like. These scientific or conceptual features are well understood and applied by most successful applied-research managers. Most of the following recommendations for improving applied-research management (and, consequently, the efficiency of information transfer to policy analysts) take into account human factors, essentially human psychological factors.

The factors may be partially explained by Murphy's Law, Maslow's Triangle, the Peter Principle, or organizational psychology, but in common terms they are the many things that human beings can do both deliberately and subconsciously to mess up a perfectly designed management system. The recommendations below, which take these factors into consideration, are tailored specifically to applied research. The same analytical process could be used to develop a set for basic research, but since the human factors in that area of science are considerably different, the recommendations would be different. The applied-research recommendations have been grouped in four categories: procedural, organizational, personality, and motivational aspects.

Before proceeding we shall take explicit notice of the fact that only two federal agencies' science transfer and applied-research systems have been reviewed in depth, and then only in the area of environmental research and policy analysis. Although it might be possible to argue that other agencies or departments, say Agriculture, Defense, or Education, have had more success than we present here, or at least different experiences (even though we made use of secondary sources to suggest that they probably have not), it is equally true that confining our discussion to information transfer in EPA and DOE gave us several opportunities for comparison, between agencies with essentially similar charters, through the reigns of several policy leaders. It is our opinion that the results would not be fundamentally altered under other circumstances or by analyzing the experiences of other agencies.

PROCEDURAL ASPECTS OF MANAGING
APPLIED RESEARCH

Examination of the EPA research planning systems and the DOE's EDP system reveals few fundamental faults with their basic organizational procedures, which are, by and large, founded on traditional "management by objective" precepts. However, we offer several points of advice respecting human factors, which will increase the probability that the system will perform as designed.

First, the procedures that the systems require of the participants should not place inordinate communication or clerical burdens on either the scientific researchers or the analysts. If these two groups spend half their time completing questionnaires and information sheets, they can only do half as much research, management, or analysis.

Second, the procedures must be endorsed, supported, tested, and used by senior executives within the organization. In short, they *must* receive management support. Because the rigor and time required to make any formal management system work as planned are not usually enjoyed by either scientists or analysts, the procedures will rapidly lapse into disuse or misuse if there is not steady top-level reinforcement.

Third, the procedures should be designed with organizational accountability and enforcement authority to ensure that all parties perform the assigned management tasks diligently. If a major party in any proposed management system can refuse to "play ball" and go unpunished, the procedure will fail catastrophically.

Fourth, procedures should recognize and respect existing formal and informal organizational power structures and avoid actions that appear to violate these structures. If an organizational structure needs to be changed so as to manage applied research more effectively, it should be formally and explicitly changed. Attempting to effect a basic organizational change in the way people do things covertly through a "new" management system is nearly always fatal.

In short, the procedures should be relatively uncomplicated, formally institutionalized, enforced, and believed important to the mission of the agency by the various parties (including management). Put another way, the system should make possible and explicit a way to accomplish an already agreed-upon agency mission.

ORGANIZATIONAL ASPECTS

One of the pervasive flaws in public sector organizations is the seemingly constant turf battle between agencies or between groups within an agency. Bureaucrats are often forced to spend too much time protecting their area of responsibility from raids by other organizational units. One way to avoid this situation is to know what one is supposed to do, what others do, and what one can expect of others. Functional responsibilities should be explicit, enforced, and consistent at all levels of management. A clear delineation of responsibility, for example, between the research staff and the analysis staff can help to eliminate many friction points in an information delivery system in a mission-oriented agency—one area of present concern. Similar nonemotional delineations for the basic-research and applied-research groups are also necessary. With each group needing the services of the other, self-interest can spur cooperation, as it does elsewhere. Let us now look at four basic functions in the transfer process with this in mind: determining research needs, priorities, and resource allocation, implementing the research, controlling the quality of the research, and evaluating the utility of the results.

Needs, Priorities, and Resources

Research needs in a mission agency should be derived primarily from the user community. This requires an effective means of communicating the needs and priorities to the research managers, and of ensuring that the requested information is actually being sought by the research programs. If the prioritizing function is now held by the basic-research units, some fluctuation of research priorities will result when others are permitted to become part of the process. This outcome may be frustrating for the research scientist, but the time mismatch between the needs of the policy community and the results obtained by the basic-science community means that at least some of the results may be wasted if careful thought is not given to the questions being addressed and the delivery time promised.

Once a system for setting research priorities is established and working in a mission-oriented agency, a procedure to ensure responsiveness is necessary, so that scarce research dollars can be efficiently used in terms of mission-oriented priorities. Part of such a procedure should be a method of examining research already under way in the light of present policy needs. Because that part of federal bureaucracy which manages research is characteristically concerned with implementing the next year's program and planning for the year after that, it sometimes fails to monitor progress carefully in the current year. The results of the current year's work and those of the previous year or two make up the scientific underpinning for feeding information into the policy stream. Finally, a small percentage of the research effort should be discretionary (planned by the scientists according to their priorities, rather than the mission agency's), so that fundamental research expected to add to the longer-term knowledge base can be carried out. This "protected zone" strategy not only placates the researchers, but allows the potential for long-term stability in a research program.

The bulk of the research funds could be allocated by using management procedures such as those employed at EPA or DOE, or by any similar management scheme. This would tend to mean the creation of a formal prioritization scheme like Zero-Based Budgeting or Strategic Planning (although EPA has evolved to a consensus-meeting format with similar results). Once again, we stress that identifying needs and then prioritizing them in the light of agency mission and available resources. These exercises are not enough in and of themselves, however. They will always be open to question and suspicion unless there are candid and frequent input and feedback between the producer and user communities. Managers hould realize that the latter process walks a fine line between keeping the client groups informed and letting them run the program.

Implementation

In the spirit of setting clear lines of functional demarcation between agency units, the research information user community should be divorced from implementation entirely. It should be the responsibility of the research manager to build and maintain an integrated program designed to answer as many of the research questions as possible for the mission agency with assigned resources at his disposal. Policy analysts and those who set regulations usually do not have professional expertise in designing experiments, selecting qualified research personnel, and evaluating their capabilities. Although it is equally true that most bureaucratic research managers do not have the time to do the research themselves, they do have the experience to ensure that others are carrying out the task in a proper manner.

Further, the choice of the performing institution (in the case of contractor or grant research projects) should not be concerned with the political or policy process. The proposal evaluation and selection mechanism, as a variation of that used in the basic-research area, is well defined and understood by the scientists and science managers and has generally functioned to bring about quality research. Allocation schemes for apportioning shares of research funds to areas of the nation on a political basis may keep politicians satisfied but offer no assurance of optimizing the output from the research dollars in terms of either product quality or agency needs. The analyst and the agency should not care where the work is done as long as research results are provided when needed.

Scientists, on the other hand, should not get deeply involved in the short-run analysis of policy issues. Neither should they define or prioritize the importance of these issues from their research perspective. They can help analysts, however, to understand the quality and meaning of their findings, since research projects rarely develop data and information that answer the original questions explicitly.

Quality Control

The peer review process of the science community—if it is narrowly confined to research veracity and how results fit into the information base already in place in the mission agency—should also remain with the research program and its science managers. As a point of fact, there is no way that anyone outside the responsible research community can perform such a task or even contribute credible input to the process of quality assurance. This type of review of the research does not consider the relevance of research results to the mission of the agency, but only their accuracy. It answers the question "Is it right?," not "Is it useful?." The latter question should be answered as part of another review process that includes evaluations by the analytical and applied-research communities.

Utility

An iterative process should take the scientific results after they are accepted in peer review and make sure that the information is useful to the policy process and, indeed, responsive to the mission agency's needs. Although it should be the science group who is responsible for the research results, the judgment on their utility ought to be reached by the user community. The scientist attests to the veracity of the research findings, but the analyst should be the one who determines whether a particular "true" statement is what is needed for analyses that contribute to the agency mission. There will also be times that the scientist and the analyst will have to take the findings of the science community and, observing the proper caveats, extend or embellish them so that they are more directly useful to the policy or regulatory issue at hand. The scientist is characteristically not willing to release a finding as "fact" until it passes all of the peer reviews of his colleagues. It would be accidental if this finding were in the exact form the analyst could use. It is part of the skills of the analyst to take these "facts" and use them to give best-case or worst-case analyses, to test the impacts of various policy choices. By definition such analyses are the best that can be done, given time and resource constraints. Within their limitations, they are accurate. They are not "facts," however.

Clearly then, the process described is one of scientific and analytical staffs constantly interacting and feeding data one to the other as research and policy analyses programs are set out and evolved in a mission agency. The neat lines of demarcation presented here are useful for a discussion purpose; the actual procedure is going to be more dynamic, spontaneous, and indistinct.

The preceding sections discussed some organizational aspects of a mission-oriented agency that uses research as input in its decision process. The fundamental differences in training and perspective between the groups that make up the research and policy analysis shops are a key to their successful management. The next sections will move away from these comparisons and generalizations and begin to address the actors themselves. Our earlier discussions spent some time with the ethos of science and the scientists; the literature is similarly biased toward the scientific model. The next sections will, therefore, discuss those who are not basic scientists but are practitioners of applied research at the extreme of answers on demand: policy analysts.

PERSONALITY CONFLICTS

This section addresses the personal requisites of effective staff members in policy analysis or issue assessment offices. Although the picture of such individuals is painted with a broad brush, the general characteristics of these people are accurate. The applied researcher, as an individual, stands somewhere in between the stereotypical scientist and the analyst and can be seen as possessing something of both groups' attributes. Policy analysts could come from almost any formal discipline, including physics, chemistry, biology, engineering, law, economics, political science, journalism, and linguistics, to name a few. The criteria for selecting a policy analysis staff must explicitly address several interpersonal and attitudinal skills and traits that are not formally taught, usually not cited on personal résumés, and frequently undetectable in a short, formal employment interviews. The following are some, not necessarily mutually exclusive, attributes of good policy analysts.

Gregariousness A policy analyst's principal function is gathering data, information, and opinions from a variety of people. Therefore, he must, in general, like to interact with people. Whereas a successful basic researcher can be shy, reserved, and solitary, a person with these personality traits usually is not a successful analyst.

Interdisciplinary Tolerance Although an effective policy analyst can come from almost any professional discipline, a key requirement is that he respect and understand the role and philosophies of other, often disparate, disciplines in order to maximize the breadth of information in the policy process. Discipline snobbery ("my professional group has all the right answers for society") is usually a fatal affliction in policy analysis. The applied scientist is apt not to be as tolerant of other disciplines as is the analyst, but is often forced outside his field to buttress the incomplete information of his parent discipline in producing information on demand. In most cases this familiarity breeds respect for others, or at least tolerance.

Inquisitiveness Because a good policy analysis tends to be relatively comprehensive and current, a good analyst must be a perpetual investigator, always on the lookout for new and different information that may be relevant to his particular policy topics. Professional antiquity is most evident and hindering in the field of policy analysis. Specialists, in the form of the scientist who spends his career on a single facet of a single discipline, are an unnecessary luxury in the fast-paced policy and regulatory worlds, where issues are amenable to technical inputs for very short periods of time, at most months, more likely days.

Responsiveness   Political questions often arise without warning and require answers on a time scale deemed unreasonable by many who do research. The effective policy analyst should recognize the reasons for this urgency and be able to manipulate available resources to respond accordingly. The applied researcher seldom would become involved in the day-to-day brushfires of the policy analyst. On the other hand, he is restricted to producing a product in the time frame specified in his contract. The scientist's answer that he will be done when he is done (if ever) is unacceptable.

Ability to Compromise   Policy analysts are continually faced with information requests of varying size, complexity, and response time. They should be able to formulate the best response possible within the available time, money, and personnel resources. Often this "best" response is an uncomfortable compromise on the depth, accuracy, precision, and reliability of the analysis, relative to what could be done with larger amounts of time and money. Again, the analyst should appreciate the need for these compromises and accept the fact that later and more exhaustive analyses might produce somewhat different results. The applied researcher differs somewhat from both the analyst and the scientist in that he has more time (and, typically, other resources) in which to bound the problem he is addressing. He is better able to specify clearly under what conditions he expects his analysis to hold. Even with such caveats, however, he is still at risk in terms of later findings of the science community.

Flexibility   A policy analyst should have not only a broad range of skills and knowledge but also the psychological ability to move quickly from one job or topic to another. He should apply himself to the issue that the public or the administration considers top priority at the moment, irrespective of his own interests, judgments, or desires. The applied research again differs only in degree and stands somewhere along the continuum between the dedicated, single-issue scientist and the analyst.

Fluency in Writing   The policy analyst's principal medium is the written word. A large portion of policy analysis consists of translating scientific information into meaningful lay terms. Analyses should be prepared in a variety of different styles and levels of detail, depending on the particular purpose and client. The successful policy analyst is a quick and careful writer who can cut through several different jargons in the physical and social sciences and produce an issue statement that can be readily telescoped up or down. But writing and presentation skills are not the monopoly of these people. Good communication is universally needed. The difference is the production speed.

Self-motivation The rewards for a successful public-sector policy analyst are few, limited principally to a continued paycheck, sometimes a verbal thank you, and in rare cases a promotion. Only within the last ten or fifteen years have there been formal professional organizations or journals of a national or international nature, and even now there is no single society that dominates this discipline. Negative reinforcement is the dominant motivation; that is, an analyst is informed quickly and clearly if his work is faulty. Repeated faulty analyses quickly erode the analyst's credibility, which might put his job at risk. Public policy analysts should be able to derive a high degree of satisfaction from their association with high-level decision-makers and being a part of important government decisions.

Public recognition is nonexistent. Information translators, facilitators, and users are considered to be in routine, simple, noncreative jobs. For example, many people still recall the names of the developers of polio vaccines (Salk, Sabin), but no one is remembered for designing and implementing the nationwide vaccination program, without which the disease could not have been effectively eliminated.

Congressional recognition and rewards in the form of sustained or increased program budget are similarly directed toward the more glamorous fields of inventing or developing new products or new information. Effective, competent use of information and implementation of new methods is simply "expected."

Like the other stereotypical characteristics discussed throughout the book, these are very dependent on personal attributes and less on formal training or job descriptions. This does not mean that only certain types of people could be analysts or that no scientist could be one. Rather, it suggests that the labels often tend to hide more than they illuminate and that people who make good scientists would, by and large, not like to be analysts and that analysts would be poorly motivated to be research scientists. Both jobs are equally professional (as are all those in between these extremes) and equally demanding—but in very different ways.

Finally, in the area of personal attributes, we turn to seeing what makes the practitioners of these professions tick and what might be done to make them tick in a more predictable fashion.

MOTIVATIONAL ASPECTS

As discussed above, a policy analyst in recent years had to be satisfied with small, private rewards or simple compliments on hard work and a job well done. This lack of formal public reward might be seen to be a major impediment to the research information transfer process. At times it renders difficult the manager's task of recruiting and retaining the types of highly talented people described in the previous section. Although the nonexistence of a mature professional society and the anonymity of the job are not quickly remedied, provisions in the Civil Service Reform Act of 1978 offer opportunities to increase the formality and effectiveness of rewards and penalties for the senior managers and executives in the federal policy analysis profession.

The federal grades at the top of the current General Schedule (GS-13 to GS-15) now are established in a fashion to:

- Make pay decisions for employees on the basis of performance.
- Recognize and encourage individual and organizational high-quality performance.
- Provide smaller pay increases when contributions lag or diminish.

Merit pay determinations must be based on an employee's performance on the job—an appraisal of that performance being the vehicle by which to recognize different levels of quality performance with different amounts of merit pay. Agencies must provide training to improve the objectivity of these appraisals and must tell employees the purpose of the system and how it works within their agency. Merit pay decisions are to be based on such factors as:

- Improvement of efficiency, productivity, and quality of work or service, including any significant reduction in paperwork.
- Cost efficiency.
- Timeliness of performance.
- Other indications of the effectiveness, productivity, and quality of performance of employees for whom the employee is responsible.
- To the extent applicable, the employee's performance in meeting affirmative action goals and equal employment opportunity requirements.

In addition to individual performance, organizational accomplishment may also be taken into account.

The federal government's Senior Executive Service also has set up an appraisal system. The Civil Service Reform Act requires that performance goals be established annually for all executives. The goal-setting process is a collaborative effort between the employee and his supervisor and includes both organizational and personal objectives. Typical areas for measurement are productivity, quality of work, promptness in performance, cost efficiency, and progress in meeting affirmative action goals.

In both cases technology transfer or research products could be explicitly set as criteria for performance appraisal. In the case of technology transfers (largely hardware) from the public to the private sectors, the greatest single factor in encouraging the public-sector research managers to sponsor research that was useful to the private sector was to change the way these managers' performance was measured. Instead of accepting research designed around "proof of product," the payoff was to be related to commercialization. This concept was tied to and monitored by the budget process and formal mechanisms called the Technology Implementation Plan (see "Proposed Solutions," Chapter 2). With the revision of the Civil Service Act in 1978, task monitoring in the public sector became even easier. All civil service managers, Grade 13 and above, are formally reviewed each year, and their raise (or bonus) or even job retention is formally tied to these reviews. The policy-maker who desires to make commercial viability a reality could cause the performance evaluations to be a function of how well the research manager achieved this goal. Similar guidance and monitoring could be instituted in the area of science managers whose output is meant to be used by an operating agency. Now the policy leader who wants to set in place a transfer or research-on-demand process has the means at his disposal of formally tasking his troops and measuring how well they do.

The principal stumbling blocks to success in this area are scientific peer review and resource adequacy. Peer review, one of the cornerstones of science, may have to be modified if it is to be used at all on applied research. As we noted in the section on organizational aspects, there are both a veracity and a utility check that have to be performed on each project. We arbitrarily divided the science mission into so-called basic and mission-oriented research. The basic phase is handled with the standard peer review process. For those portions of the science program that are meant to be responsive to an agency's needs, the review group should be a mix of those who would attest to the truth or accuracy of the research output and those who would attest to its utility in the agency's mission. The latter group's function would be somewhat broader than just performing the normal discipline-oriented peer review of scientific work. The same group would also oversee the research program for reliability and quality.

These generalizations of the scientist and the analyst are a useful bit of insight for those who are trying to understand why such change is not more automatic and what kind of management structure and follow-through would be necessary to make it so. The next section will build on these characteristics and describe one system which would successfully implement a transfer process and manage a research-on-demand system.

DELIVERING RESEARCH AS A PRODUCT

The role of the manager has always been pretty much the same regardless of whether he is in the public or private sector or what subject he is managing in those sectors. He sets responsibility, creates organization structure, authority lines, and process flow, manages personnel in all its aspects, sets quality standards and controls for them, handles financial management, and plans work, control, and communication. No matter what the organization, these functions have to be carried out. It is our contention that in the area of applied science, once the existing rigidities are understood, the process of delivering science can be done in a more or less straightforward fashion. An article in the *Public Administration Review*[1] suggested a perspective of science as a system of production. We shall make use of this concept here. The system, as presented in the article, goes through a series of steps, from the development of an idea to the evaluation of a formal result.

The Need

Almost all agencies that sponsor research and development picture the responsibility for need definition as belonging to the program manager. It seldom is that neat in actual operation. At times the need is specified in legislation; at others the need is generated from other parts of the agency that house the research group; at still others the research or engineering community may specify needs based on what they know of the state of the art of the disciplines used to fulfill a companion or related policy need.

For most mission agencies there should be little excuse for any real surprises, in terms of not knowing a goodly portion of the research and development that will be needed through time. Characteristically, in regulatory agencies (such as the EPA) the standards, regulations, or enforcements growing out of legislation or legal actions contain and create timetables by which research findings will be in demand. These legislatively mandated requirements should have a first priority in any resource-ranking scheme. As a matter of fact, these legal requirements are useful, not only to the regulatory agency in carrying out their mission, but also to the manager, by enhancing his ability and responsibility to ensure that required research be done in time for the input to be useful.

Any format could be adopted for users to request the projects. It should include such things as who wants the results, what specifically is needed, and by what time. There should be considerable effort dedicated to understanding what is wanted and to the desired format.

Project Selection

Once all these needs get to the program manager, a system must be utilized to rank them by need and amount of information within a particular need. The public and private sectors are replete with such systems. The selecting can be done by just the program manager, by just the in-house staff, by in-house and outside experts, by "peers," or by quantitative method, or by some combination of these.

In addition to these nonquantified methods, there are some generalized analytic systems. In the main, these systems are structured so that projects in the selection grouping are assigned a numerical value by one or more knowledgeable persons. The projects are then combined by some analytic method and, finally, ranked according to some specified algorithm.

There are several possible methods of actually performing a quantitative selection. Some methods specify a number of problems that should be solved by the project (cost, probability of success, timeliness, etc.), and a score and/or weight is assigned to each. The display of these combined scores on each project after they are summed automatically ranks them in the range of those with the highest score (best) to those with the lowest (least desirable).

Another group of techniques comes in the kit bag of the economist. These include cost—benefit, cost effectiveness, and most profitable project. Again, a comparison of the ratios or profits of the candidate projects results in a more or less automatic prioritization.

Finally, a form of mathematical optimization can be used if there exists sufficient data to specify the problem. By definition, if each project is correctly specified to fit the algorithm, it will calculate the best set of them to accomplish a given objective (given constraints such as budget).

Even with all these methods, the analytic tools are but one input to the funding decision process. On the one hand, they give rigor and consistency to the project selection process. On the other, they force projects which are often quite dissimilar to fit a standard mold— sometimes to the point where the results of the exercise are meaningless. Such techniques might be used by a bureaucratic manager for no other reason than to convince people that he has been rigorous and thorough in his stewardship of entrusted federal funds.

Research Design

With the funding organization clearly in the role of specifying what research it wants and when it wants results, there is a question of who specifies in the plan how the analysis will be conducted. There is no question what the response would be from the science community. Since they are both the area and technical experts, they would feel that they should have the say on the research design and strategy. On the other hand, all areas of science are not noncontroversial as to subject matter and technique. The use of certain methods, data, theories has a great deal to do with the final result. This makes the question of project design quite problematical. No reputable scientist would carry out a project he did not believe was accurately specified or conformed to his best judgment of what should be done and how it should be; to do otherwise would place him in the role of an intellectual prostitute. The user, however, has the right to protect himself from being the victim of a scientist's pet theory. In some instances, where there is known divisiveness in the science community on a particular topic, several approaches might be tried, time and resources permitting. If not, then a process of negotiation may have to be resorted to, in which the sensitivities of both scientist and user are considered in such a way that the output is in a form that satisfies both. Carefully qualified and caveated reports are usually the solution.

Resource Allocation

Several factors have to be considered in the area of resource allocation. They include how the finances are to be provided, what the cost of the project should be, how many people and what combination of disciplines should work on it.

The question of how a project should be funded is involved with factors that include whether it should be performed by federal researchers or funded as a grant or contract. Because the output can be specified, and because the user wants to maintain control over the product, the contract is the preferred instrument. But this is only a part of the picture. The contract could be written for work over a period of years, with interim outputs, or it could specify a single output at the end of a time period. If the output is expected to be a series of related products, but all the individual products cannot be explicitly specified until some date in the future, then a task order contract could be employed which allows for detailed specification of each stage as it becomes due.

The desired form and content of the output from the research project is apt to change as the policy issue shifts focus and emphasis during performance of the research. To accommodate these changes, the contract should be written in several phases, so that mid-course redirection is possible. A useful first phase should be a state-of-the-art survey and a detailed work plan with expected output at ensuing stages.

The individuals assigned to projects of this sort will change with the research organization. It is not unusual, especially when the laboratories are ones that were originally developed to be research arms of a federal agency, that basic scientists who are "burned out" or who want a change for some other reason are resuscitated as applied scientists. In the regulatory field (both EPA and DOE are examples) the research labs were originally set up to provide largely basic research and development for, say, the atomic energy or water pollution missions of the original bureaucracies, before they were combined with other pieces of mission agencies to make the present departments. The research managers and the laboratory scientists almost always have a considerable difficulty switching under circumstances of mission shift, and a considerable effort (and friction) is expended as the agenda are moved from basic to applied research. The final shift usually is not successful until there is a change in the research and, often, management personnel.

Although it should be straightforward, trying to price a research and development project in terms of both money and time is always a chore. To some extent, if the research is to provide the technical backup for a regulation, then there is no question when the results are needed, as that is legally specified. In the main, the situation is "give me whatever you can on this issue by a specified date." As we have already noted, this kind of request is exactly what a basic scientist does not want to respond to. He does not want to deliver a finding that he is not absolutely sure of and which has not been thoroughly peer-reviewed. With or without caveats, a less than totally checked-out finding has no place in the world of pure science. In spite of the reticence of pure science, though, the partial information of ongoing basic science is needed in the regulatory policy process, and someone will provide it or will produce input for the decision without the newest data. A decision will be made, though, and will not await science.

The cost of delivering scientific results on demand depends upon several factors: how much is already known about the issue, how much time is available (which indirectly determines how many people will be needed for the project), what other equipment and computer assistance will be required, and the like. Even a cursory look at experience with past accuracy in estimating public contract costs reveals that the estimates of these costs have been pretty inaccurate. A painstaking process of estimating the resources needed, from the bottom up, task by task, is the most promising way of getting the best guess. But even this method is influenced heavily by past experience and ability. Looking at the previous job experience of the bidder suggests that companies who have done large jobs overestimate; smaller, underestimate. But, in general, there is a very human tendency to underestimate, since everyone wants to please, and assuring the customer that something can be done within a budget (even when the odds are that nothing can be) is such an attempt. Washington has an expression for bidding on proposals called "lie and try," which is the extreme of this tendency.

Other factors enter into the costing equation than the size of the job, the state of the art of the related scientific field, and the experience of the group or firm doing the work. In general, these are all concerned with the experience of the research outfit in reference to the particular question being asked. In the public sector those agencies that work as a matter of course with in-house laboratories have the least potential for resource estimation problems, because of the familiarity of managers with each other between agency and laboratory. Those who contract out have the greatest risk of making or accepting poor estimates.

PRODUCING THE PRODUCT

Ordinarily the actual research management on a day-to-day basis is not something the public agency managers become directly involved with. As long as the research is of high quality and produced in an efficient and timely fashion, there is little incentive to become interested. On the other hand, there are situations in which the question of how the research is being produced becomes important. If the work is not going well, then there may be a need to "step in." Or, if the agency staff is intimately involved in the work, then more frequent interaction may come to pass. Because the funder has the authority that comes with providing the cash for the project (called the Golden

Rule: he who has the gold, rules), he may become a de facto project leader. The extreme of this situation is one in which the contract researchers become a part of an in-house team effort and function as a "body shop" or technical "stable" for a public sector group.

USE OF EVALUATION

In a typical research sequence, the final stage is one at which the users are identified and the product is prepared for their use. In the regulatory and policy areas these users are clearly identified, as is the form in which the product is needed. Characteristically, the sponsor is the user and the form of the results is specified in the original request.

This leaves one of the most important features of managing research and development for the last. To organize this discussion, we shall make use of a table developed by Keaton;[2] see Table 3. According to his outline, five categories of program management evaluation range from "show and tell" to financing, to program, to technical workshop, to problem search. The first is useful only as an introduction, and the last is likely never to be useful for our purposes. The program review is the one that most agency personnel at the management level are subjected to and are familiar with. It allows reporting the status of a program at various times and comparing it with the agreed-upon program. Mid-course corrections are discussed and implemented when necessary.

The financial workshop is highly specialized and not normally a production review mode. The technical workshop is a good strategy at the beginning of an effort or when the project has run into a snag. Again, this is a specialized technique and definitely not part of a normal review procedure.

The total process outlined in the last several pages has given us a procedure that the agency and research managers can follow from the beginning to the end of a project and already do, to some extent or other. The steps are fairly straightforward and do lend themselves to implementation. It is possible to require that research be produced on demand, with the caveat that not everything we want to know about the issue will be available at decision time. But that is the nature of any engineering or applied-research project. What can be expected is the best output possible at a point in time. The difficulties, as we have already noted, are normally the result of a failure to understand the realities of the roles for each of the actors. We have addressed these difficulties and suggested some remedies to balance demands, expectations, and needs. Let us turn to these again in summary form.

Table 3
Five Categories of Program Evaluation

	Show and tell	Financial review	Program review	Technical workshop	Problem search
Purpose	To convey general information	Compare expenditures with budget	Compare status of program with plan	Address technical problems and search for solutions	Find problems in a program and determine solutions
Characteristics Overview		Financial experts ask questions	Accountable individuals (managers) are informed of the program status in an interactive manner	Technical experts exchange information	Accountable individuals ask questions
	Little technical and budget information conveyed	Nontechnical discussion	Progress is compared with a predetermined plan	Potential technical pitfalls or blind alleys are examined	Technical managerial financial problems are examined
	Marketing or public-relations-oriented	Cash in, cash out examination	Variances from the plan are noted for later attention	"Workshop" atmosphere	Project leader is usually on the defensive
	Speaker (i.e., project leader) is "in charge"		Mutually supportive atmosphere prevails		Mutual lack of trust

Resulting Action May influence thinking of the audience	Adjust expenditure rate	If problems have surfaced, techniques and tools are sought, to assist the project leader in finding solutions discussed and agreed upon Plan is revised as discussed Cycle continues: Plan → organize → implement → review → plan → etc.	Technical solutions are recommended Plans are changed accordingly	Project leader is often expected to implement "armchair designs" Project leader may be removed Project may be stopped

*From P. W. Keaton, "Five Ways to Review R&D Programs," *Research Management*, September 1980.

RECAPITULATION AND SUMMARY

Our work here makes a contribution to the public administration literature—not by designing, modifying, or recombining a specific institutionalized method of transferring scientific findings from the "halls" of research to the policy formulation or regulatory stream, or for developing a catchy new management scheme. Our procedural and organizational sections essentially take the posture that many different schemes could be either modified or designed de novo to handle scientific-information management and transfer in a mission agency, but that each must at least cover the goals and requirements described above. More to the point, the significant message is that care must be exercised to find the right kind of staff, motivate it, and manage it formally, so that they have both the ability and the desire to transfer and manage research requirements and findings effectively. Care must be taken to ensure that the goal of transference or management of research-on-demand is institutionally possible and efficient and that dedicated people who want to do the job are involved. In short, the institutional change that must come to pass is not necessarily one that redesigns an organizational plan, but one which restructures the professional reward and motivational system. As such, workers who are motivated by particular rewards will respond to such inducements. Those who are not will automatically be motivated to seek employment elsewhere. The latter result is in contradiction to current proclivities, which are to change an organizational plan so it will respond to almost all external pressures. The change, unless it also impacts the professional level's goals and rewards, is likely to be an unsuccessful strategy. Our suggestions are simple, or at least strightforward, but are the type seldom implemented in a modern bureaucracy, which seems to prefer reorganization as its favorite pastime.

REFERENCES

1. Richard Mason, "The Role of Management in Science," *Public Administration Review*, March/April, 1979.

2. P. W. Keaton, "Five Ways to Review R&D Programs," *Research Management*, September 1980.

Bibliography

Ansoff, I. H., "Evaluation of Applied Research in a Business Firm," in J. R. Bright (ed.), *Research, Development and Technological Innovation*, Richard Irwin, Homewood, Illinois, 1964.

Bailey, R. E., and B. T. Jensen, "Troublesome Transition from Scientist to Manager," *Personnel*, Vol. 42, September 1965.

Blake, Stewart P., *Managing for Responsive Research and Development*, W. H. Freeman and Company, San Francisco, California.

Boffey, Philip M., *The Brain Bank of America*, McGraw Hill, New York, 1975.

Broad, William J., "Would-Be Academician Pirates Papers," *Science*, Vol. 208, June 27, 1980.

Cole, Jonathan R., and Stephen Cole, "The Ortega Hypothesis," *Science*, Vol. 178, October 22, 1972.

Council on Environmental Quality, *Environmental Quality—1980*, U.S. Government Printing Office, Washington, D.C., 1981.

Drucker, Peter, "Science and Industry, Challenges of Antagonistic Interdependence," *Science*, Vol. 204, May 25, 1979.

Frame, J. Davidson, "Sixteen Year Trends in Biomedical Funding and Publication," contract report submitted to the National Institutes of Health, March 15, 1980.

Frame, J. Davidson, "Science Indicators in Science Policy Formulation: The Case of the United States," presented at an international conference on "Evaluation in Science and Technology: Theory and Practice," Dubrovnik, Yugoslavia, June 30 to July 4, 1980.

Gee, Edwin A., and Chaplin Tyler, *Managing Innovation*, Wiley & Sons, New York, 1978.

Hippel, Eric A. von, "Users as Innovators," *Technology Review*, Vol. 80, January 1978.

Hollomon, J. Herbert, et al., *Government Involvement in the Innovation Process*, Office of Technology Assessment, Washington, D.C., 1978.

Holmfeld, John D., "Science Indicators and Other Indicators: Some User Observations," *4S*, Vol. 3, Fall 1978.

House, Peter W., and David W. Jones, *Getting It Off the Shelf, A Methodology for Implementing Federal Research*, Westview Press, Boulder, Colorado, 1976.

House, Peter W., and Dario R. Monti, *Using Futures Forecasting in the Planning Process: A Case Study of the Energy-Environment Interface*, U.S. Department of Energy, Office of Technology Assessments, Office of the Assistant Secretary for Environment, April 1979.

International Council of Scientific Unions, *1979 Year Book*, Paris, France, 1979.

International Institute of Applied Systems Analysis, *Annual Report 1977*, Vienna, Austria, 1978.

Kaplan, Abraham, *The Conduct of Inquiry*, Chandler, Scranton, Pennsylvania, 1964.

Keaton, P. W., "Five Ways to Review R&D Programs," *Research Management*, September 1980.

Kiren, Michael, "Science vs. Government. A Reconsideration," *Policy Science*, Vol. 12, Elsevier Scientific Publishing Company, Amsterdam, 1980.

Knott, J., and A. Wildavsky, "If Dissemination is the Solution, What is the Problem?", *Knowledge, Creation, Diffusion, Utilization*, Vol. I, No. 4, Sage Publications, Inc., June 1980.

Koontz, Harold, and Cyril O'Donnell, *Essentials of Management* (2nd ed.), McGraw-Hill, New York, 1978.

Kuhn, Thomas, *The Structure of Scientific Revolutions*, University of Chicago Press, Chicago, Illinois, 1962.

Mason, R. O., "The Role of Management in Science," *Public Administration Review*, Mar/Apr 1979.

Merton, Robert K., "The Normative Structure of Science," *The Sociology of Science*, University of Chicago Press, Chicago, Illinois, 1973.

Miles, R., Jr., "The Origin and Meaning of Miles' Law," *Public Administration Review*, No. 38, 1978.

MITRE Corporation, "Task Force Report on Health Effects Assessment," prepared for the Acting Assistant Secretary for Environment, U.S. Department of Energy, August 1978.

Muller, R. A., "Innovation and Scientific Funding," *Science*, Vol. 209, August 22, 1980.

Myers, Sumner, and Eldon E. Sweezy, "Why Innovations Fail," *Technology Review*, Vol. 80, March/April 1978.

National Archives Records Service, GSA, *U.S. Government Manual*, U.S. Government Printing Office, Washington, D.C., May 1980.

Organization of Economic Co-Operation and Development, *Management of Research and Development*, Istanbul, Turkey.

Peter, L. J., *The Peter Principle: Why Things Go Wrong*, Bantam Books, New York, 1970.

Price, Derek de Solla, *Science Since Babylon (Enlarged Edition)*, Yale University Press, New Haven, Connecticut, 1976.

Reagan, Michael, *Science and the Federal Patron*, Oxford University Press, New York, 1969.

Roman, Daniel D., *Science, Technology, and Innovation*, Grid Publishing Company, Columbus, Ohio, 1980.

Sander, William F., "Promoting an Effective R&D/Marketing Interface," *Research Management*, July 1980.

Sauder, W. E., *Management Decisions Methods for Managers of Engineering and Research*, Holt, Reinhold, and Winston Company, New York, 1978.

Schmookler, Jacob, *The Sources of Invention*, Harvard University Press, Cambridge, Massachusetts, 1966.

Simon, Herbert, A., "Theories of Decision-Making in Economics and Behavioral Science," *American Economic Review*, June 1959.

Storer, Norman W., "The Internationality of Science and the Nationality of Scientists," *International Social Science Journal*, Vol. 22, 1970.

Thomsen, Dietrick F., "Will Astronomy Go Into Orbit?", *Science News*, Vol. 118, August 30, 1980.

Twiss, Brian, *Managing Technological Innovation*, Longman Group Ltd., London, 1974.

U.S. Department of Energy, "Review of the EDP Program," Staff Paper, Office of Technology Impacts, Office of Environment, January 3, 1978.

U.S. Department of Energy, "Program and Project Management System for DOE Outlay Program," Interim Policy and Guidance, May 31, 1978.

U.S. Department of Energy, "EDP's and PPPS," Memorandum from T. Snyder to J. Janis, August 10, 1978.

U.S. Department of Energy, "Environmental Development Plans," Order 5420.1, August 10, 1978 (supercedes Interim Management Directive No. 5102, January 15, 1978).

U.S. Department of Energy, "Environmental Planning and Review in Relation to Major Systems Acquisition Projects," memorandum from the Assistant Secretary for Environment to the Assistant Secretaries for Resource Applications, Energy Technology, and Conservation and Solar Applications, December 18, 1978.

U.S. Department of Energy, *Strategy Plan*, Office of Environment, Draft, March 1980.

U.S. Energy Research and Development Administration, "Requirement for an Environmental Development Plan (EDP)," ERDA Immediate Action Directive No. 1500.4, December 14, 1976.

U.S. Environmental Protection Agency, Office of Research and Development, "Program Planning and Reporting Manual," Washington, D.C., January 1974.

U.S. Environmental Protection Agency, Office of Research and Development, *U.S. Environmental Protection Agency Environmental Research Outlook, FY 1976 thru 1980. Report to Congress*, ORD, EPA-600/9-76-003, 1976.

U.S. General Accounting Office, "Opportunities to Fully Integrate Environmental Research and Development into Developing Energy Technologies," EMD-78-43, April 6, 1978.

Weinberg, Alvin, "Criteria for Scientific Choice," *Minerva*, Vol. I, Winter 1963.

Wert, J., A. Lieberman, and R. Levian, *R&D Management. Methods Used by Federal Agencies*, Lexington Books, D. C. Heath and Company, Lexington, Massachusetts, 1975.

NEEDS SYSTEM OF THE ENVIRONMENTAL PROTECTION AGENCY*

Each Program Area Strategy is to contain the following components:

- A list of the various Media Goals that must be achieved within the Program Area.

- A summary description of each Program Area Objective (including planned accomplishment dates recommended by the Program Area Manager for inclusion within the Program Area). Each Program Area Objective could be composed of one or more specific outputs as described by Environmental Research Objective Statements.

- A matrix that identifies and relates Program Area Objectives to the Media Goals identified above.

- A graphic indication of the time-phase relationships between the various proposed Program Area Objectives and the Media Goals.

- A numerical priority list of all Environmental Research Objective Statements recommended by the Program Area Manager.

*Environmental Protection Agency, Office of Research and Development, *Program Planning and Reporting Manual* (Washington, D.C., January 1974), pp. 10–12.

119

- A narrative discussion of the rationale supporting the indicated Environmental Research Objective Statement priorities, including a justification of any recommended Environmental Research Objective Statement that does not directly support a Program Area Objective. (These might include responses to high-priority needs that may not be directly related to strategic plans.)

Examples of objectives defined by an Environmental Research Objective Statement might include the following:

- Developing the scientific information of the type, quality, and quantity needed to solve a specific regulatory problem, such as the setting of effluent or emission standards for a given pollutant.

- Developing process technology having particular performance characteristics, operating features, and cost requirements to solve a specific control problem (e.g., control of thermal discharges from fossil-fuel power plants).

- Developing a defined level of basic scientific competence in a selected research area offering potential for future environmental applications.

- Answering a fundamental scientific question upon which an Agency policy might be based.

- Developing a device of specific cost and operating characteristics to measure a pollutant with defined precision, accuracy, and reliability.

The Research Objective Achievement Plan fulfilled several essential planning functions, specifically:

- Created the formal documentation required to allow review and evaluation of a proposed research plan.

- Provided the basis for formulating and justifying budget submissions for various Office of Research and Development programs and components to the Administrator, Office of Management and Budget, and Congress.

- Provided information on the future resource implications of initiating the pursuit of a given research objective.

- Provided research planning data and related resource requirements that became the basis for issuance of allowances at the time implementation of approved research was undertaken.

- Provided records of past resources expended and results accomplished, which could be used for assessing progress to date.

- Provided milestone data against which status of work could be assessed.

- Served (along with its corresponding Environmental Research Objective Statement) as a decision unit that could be compared with other decision units for management decisions regarding priority, cost effectiveness, etc.

- Provided a basis for informing potential grantees and contractors of specific tasks to be undertaken.

- Served as a vehicle for relating the ongoing research activities of the Office of Research and Development to specific objectives and for providing feedback of progress and results to the user community.

Each task within a Research Objective Achievement Plan defined a specific effort having a defined project that made an essential contribution to attaining the objective of the Environmental Research Objective Statement. A task was further characterized by having to be carried out under a single individual's supervision; this means that a task could not be carried out under more than one contract, grant, or interagency agreement or by more than one in-house organization. Milestone events and associated target dates were designated in each Research Objective Achievement Plan, to permit assessment of the rate of progress being made toward the final objective.

APPENDIX B

ACCOMPLISHMENTS OF THE FIRST-GENERATION ENVIRONMENTAL DEVELOPMENT PLANS*

In March 1978 an attempt was made by the Department of Energy to pull together into one document** the pertinent information of a comparative nature for each technology in a way that would be useful for planning and policy purposes and to overcome the limitation of the initial documents that they were inconsistent in their treatment of the subject matter.

The Environmental Development Plan (EDP) summaries were concentrated into a set of three tables. The first brought together certain characteristics of the 26 technologies covered: development status, facility type, geographic focus, and dependence on other emerging technologies:

---

*Peter W. House and Dario R. Monti, *Using Futures Forecasting in the Planning Process: A Case Study of the Energy-Environment Interface,* U.S. Department of Energy, Office of the Assistant Secretary for Environment, Office of Technology Impacts, April 1979, pp. 22–25.

**"Summary and Status of Environmental Development Plans," Department of Energy, Office of the Assistant Secretary for Environment, March 1978.

- Development status: Distinguished technologies according to near-term (present to 1985), middle-term (1985–2000), and long-term (beyond 2000) projects.

- Facility type: Indicated whether a technology was centralized (large-scale, limited number of sites) or distributed (smaller scale, numerous sites).

- Geographic focus: Defined locational constraints associated with the development of technology.

- Dependence on emerging technologies: Identified other developments that might be critical for successful development and commercialization of the energy technology.

The second set of tables documented potential environmental concerns associated with each technology option. The environmental concerns were classified under seven headings: air, water, land, ecology, health and safety, socioeconomic, and critical resources. Other concerns unique to the nuclear program were special nuclear materials, accountability, safeguards, and nonproliferation. Although the concerns identified in the EDP's were the traditional ones associated with energy development and end use (e.g., noxious combustion gases and land and water availability), many other special concerns have been identified, especially for new and advanced technologies.

Most of the EDP's identified environmental legislation that could affect technology development, and properly cited compliance with environmental legislation, standards, and regulations as a concern to be addressed by environmental research programs.

The third set of tables listed some of the more critical environmental research and development requirements associated with the technologies. Some of these are site-specific, some are process-specific, and others support several processes or technologies. The requirements were described in various levels of detail, depending upon the stage of technological development and the specific nature of the technology options they addressed.

Required research and assessment activities usually correlated with specific environmental concerns in each EDP. This correlation exemplifies the environmental strategies being pursued to identify or mitigate the major environmental problems of the technologies.

The resolution of complex energy-related environmental concerns requires the application of diverse scientific disciplines and the development of integrated research programs. The environmental requirements for all environmental research requirements were then usually discussed only in terms of the environmental concerns they addressed.

Besides scheduling environmental research, many of the FY 1977 EDP's also identified decision points that should be supported with Environmental Impact Assessments or Environmental Impact Statements required by the National Environmental Policy Act implementing regulations.

APPENDIX **C**

ENVIRONMENTAL DEVELOMENT PLAN PROCESS*

THE PROCESS

In a summary fashion Figure C-1 indicates the major events, information flows, and responsibilities of, and related activities external to, the proposed Environmental Development Plan process. The following description supplements the diagram.

The Environmental Development Plan (EDP) process assumed the existence of a formal indication of the relative priority of DOE energy programs. The principal input for this prioritization scheme was a DOE position assembled by the energy programs and the Assistant Secretary for Policy and Evaluation. The scheme allowed an emphasis to be placed on certain EDP's and thus helped to focus the environmental activities of the Office of Environment (and others).

Technology Description
EDP Joint Energy Programs' Assistant Secretaries
and Office of Technology Overview Activity

The preparation of the EDP began with an examination of the full technology descriptions and milestone schedules for the major (prior-

---

*Peter W. House and Dario R. Monti, *Using Futures Forecasting in The Planning Process: A Case Study of the Energy-Environment Interface,* Department of Energy, Office of the Assistant Secretary for Environment, Office of Technology Impacts, April 1979.

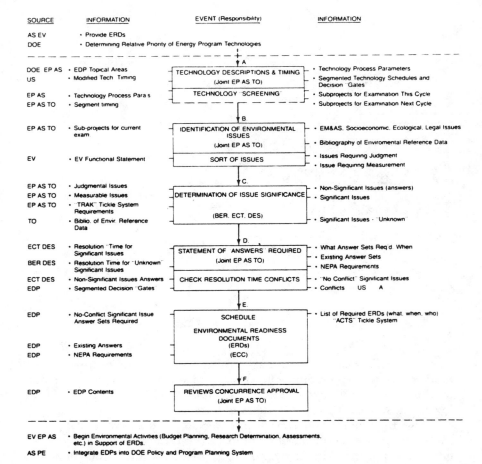

Figure C-1. Environmental Development Plan (EDP) process. A,   ; "ACTS," Action Control and Tracking System; AS, Assistant Secretary; BER, Office of Biological and Environmental Research; ECC, Environmental Coordinating Committee; ECT, Office of Environmental Control Technology; EH&S, environment, health, and safety; EP, Energy Program (generic); ERD, Environmental Readiness Document; EV, Office of Environment; NEPA, National Environmental Policy Act; OES, Office of Operational Environment and Safety; PE, Office of Planning and Evaluation; TO, Technology Overview; US, Under Secretary.

ity) program areas. The examination was a joint activity conducted by the energy programs' Assistant Secretaries and the Division of Technology Overview. The examination yielded the segmentation of the technology timing schedules into major development stages; and, for the current and next segments, sufficient engineering and technical development stages allowed the identification of the budget authorization decision points that preceded each particular development stage. These decision points or gates are points in time where the Office of Environment made a statement on the environmental "readiness" of a particular program to proceed to the next gate.

For certain priority technology program areas containing many subprojects, components, or process options, a screening procedure was applied, based on the technology descriptions for the segments preceding the next gate. Primary output of this step was the identification of particular subprojects or components to be examined environmentally in detail within the EDP currently being written. Ancillary output was an early indication of which subprojects merited detailed consideration in the EDP review process.

Identification of Environmental Issues
EDP Joint Energy Programs' Assistant Secretaries
and Division of Technology Overview Activity

For each priority technology program area or screened subprojects, a comprehensive list of potential environmental issues (concerns, barriers) was developed. "Environmental" was defined to include public and occupational health and safety, socioeconomic, ecological, and legal factors. At this point a supporting bibliography of available technology-related environmental reference data (including existing standards and regulations, potentially relevant federal inventory projects, emissions and effects data, technology assessments, etc.) was compiled.

Based on any applicable standards, regulations, and guidelines, the list of issues was sorted into (1) issues requiring a judgment (of health and safety effects) to determine the significance and importance or severity and (2) issues whose significance could be determined by measurement against a standard or guideline. (Note that a single technology subproject may generate both types.)

Determination of Importance
Office of Environment, Division of Biomedical
    and Environmental Research, Division of
    Environmental Control Technology, Division
    of Operational and Environmental Safety
    Activity

The determination of the importance and significance of the sorted issues was made by the Office of Environment divisions: "judgmental" issues in most cases went to Division of Biomedical and Environmental Research and Division of Operational and Environmental Safety, "measurable" issues to the Division of Environmental Control Technology and Division of Operational and Environmental Safety. The EDP "Joint Energy Programs' Assistant Secretaries and Division of Technology Overview Group" provided the appropriate bibliographic reference data to the Office of Environment divisions as well as the reply (time, format) requirements to DOE's Action Coordination and Tracking System ("tickle" system). The Office of Environment's importance and significance determination yields (1) nonsignificant issues—technology meets standards or has nonsevere effects, (2) significant issues—exceeds standards but may be controlled or has potentially severe effects, (3) significant issues—unknown (no characterization, measurement, or monitoring data, or severity unknown). For both of the significant-issue types, estimates of the research time required to provide a sufficient answer to (or "resolve") the issue were provided by the Office of Environment divisions.

Statement of Actions (Answers) Required
EDP Joint Energy Programs' Assistant Secretaries
    and Division of Technology Overview Activity

The EDP preparers compiled the "resolution" time estimates for the significant issues into common time periods. Primary outputs were the sets of answers required and their common lead times, as well as the set of existing answers (e.g., nonsignificant issues). National Environmental Policy Act requirements also were scheduled in this phase. A comparison of the timing of the sets of deliverable answers to the next decision gate produced (1) no-conflict significant issues if answers could be provided prior to the next gate and (2) conflict significant issues indicating potential delays in the technology development stage following the gate. The conflict situations were forwarded to the Under Secretary for resolution.

Schedule of Environmental Readiness Documents
Environmental Coordinating Committee

A formal mechanism (the EDP) was needed for the Assistant Secretary for Environment to assess the environmental readiness (adequacy and progress) of the energy program technology, so as to move to the next development stage. The Environmental Readiness Document (ERD) was an internal DOE document, principally for the use of the Assistant Secretary for Environment, that contained the environmental readiness recommendations of the Office of Environment line divisions (even though others may conduct the supporting environmental research and provided the basic documentation). In essence, a "positive" ERD would indicate that all of the significant issues associated with a technology's current (and past) development stage had been resolved.

The vehicle for scheduling the ERD mechanism was the Environmental Coordinating Committee (co-chaired by Energy Programs' Assistant Secretaries, Division of Technology Overview) with full Office of Environment division-related energy programs' Assistant Secretaries membership. The Environmental Coordinating Committee has two functions related to ERD's: (1) to schedule ERD's (define content areas, responsibility for production, and time schedule) prior to, in most cases, the next decision gate, and (2) to monitor document preparation progress and present summary statements. Function 1 was accomplished through the Environmental Coordinating Committee forum with the following as inputs: the no-conflict significant issue sets, the existing-answer nonsignificant issue sets, available or scheduled documents of the National Environmental Policy Act, and applicable reference bibliography materials. Function (2) was assisted by inserting the schedule of ERD's into the DOE Action Coordination and Tracking System ("tickle system").

Environmental Development Plan Approval
(EDP Joint Energy Programs' Assistant Secretaries
**   and Office of Technology Overview Activity**

With the completion of the ERD schedule (and/or inclusion of document summary statements) the EDP was ready for formal concurrence or approval. The major products (excluding the technology descriptions) of future EDP's was then:

- The nonsignificant issues and the ERD summary for the significant issues associated with the current technology development stage.

- The nonsignificant issues and the ERD and National Environ-

mental Policy Act (NEPA) schedule for the significant issues associated with the next technology development stage.

After approval, activities in support of ERD production began
(budget planning, research determination, regional and environment, health, and safety assessments, etc.), carried out by the Office
of Environment and the Energy Programs' Assistant Secretaries; in
support of ERD and the EDP's were integrated into DOE's Policy
and Program Planning System by the Assistant Secretary for Policy
and Evaluation.

On the basis of EDP input, and using the scheduled ERD as a
"driver," the Office of Environment line division evaluated the quality
and scope of existing research, determining their own research needs,
and with the research determined the "unit" effects (damage functions, etc., for a single technological unit). Given the unit effects
(Office of Environment, Division of Biomedical and Environmental
Research, Division of Environmental Control Technology, Division
of Operational and Environmental Safety) and policy guidance, known
impacts data (Division of Environmental Impacts), existing NEPA
documents (Office of NEPA Coordination), and the deployment
scenarios (Assistant Secretary for Policy and Evaluation, Energy Programs' Assistant Secretaries, Management Review Control Documents, others), the scheduling of Regional Impact Assessments
(Division of Regional Assessments), Health and Safety Assessments
(Division of Biomedical and Environmental Research), Intertech-
nology Assessments (Division of Environmental Impacts), and Intra-
technology Assessments (Division of Technology Overview) were
undertaken. With the assessment results, the Division of Regional
Assessments and the Assistant Secretary for Policy and Evaluation
would investigate the policy implications. All the synthesis and Office
of Environment planning implications of these research requests were
handled by the Office of Planning Coordination. (Similar processes
would occur in the energy programs.)

PROGRAM AND PROJECT MANAGEMENT SYSTEM*

PROGRAM PLANS

Each principal outlay program (funded program) line manager of the Department of Energy (DOE) developed plans for his own program. The designation of required program plans was made by the Under Secretary on the basis of recommendations and advice from program and staff organizations. The plans emphasized program strategies and the translation of general policy guidance into specific programmatic terms covering a multiyear period. The program plan was a goal-oriented description of specific technical, environmental, economic, and supporting efforts that, when brought to successful fruition, would result in significant contribution to national energy needs. The strategy was shaped over a number of years and incorporated regulatory, fiscal, or other initiatives, to complement the main scientific or technical thrust.

All the program plans have some common elements; on the other

---

*Peter W. House and Dario R. Monti, *Using Futures Forecasting in the Planning Process: A Case Study of the Energy-Environment Interface,* Department of Energy, Office of the Assistant Secretary for Environment, Office of Technology Impacts, April 1979.

hand, some elements may be unique to a particular program. Decision points, milestones, and events should be laid out in an overall program activity schedule. Each program plan was supposed to do the following.

Estimate the total cost of the program and the potential benefits and impacts.

Describe the relationships of the federal effort to related activities in the private sector.

Specify the criteria to be used for evaluating program effectiveness:

- Technical and economic performance characteristics that would constitute program success

- Milestones and other quantitative factors that could serve as a measure of program effectiveness

- Probabilities of technical success for each discrete step of the research and development process

Estimate the annual out-year costs of the program.

Describe the proposed management plan and indicate the role of contractors and participants.

Briefly describe the major environmental and socioeconomic impediments to wide-scale commercial application and the strategy for dealing with them.

Describe, where appropriate, the "commercialization" plan for the technology, plans for transfer to other DOE entities or the market, and the implementation schedule; include statements of technical readiness for each appropriate technology application or system (where the major technical problems that are the major impediments to commercialization will be resolved).

When the programs encompassed more than one technology or alternative technologies or concepts (for example, the Coal Gasification Program contains a number of alternative processes, producing a variety of fuels), each specific technology was addressed as indicated, and the relationship and dependence among technologies were described. Specific issues and their resolution, which were implicit assumptions in the plan, were identified.

ENERGY SYSTEM ACQUISITION
PROJECT PLAN

The baseline document for DOE project activities is the Energy System Acquisition Project Plan (ESAPP). This plan covers the project from initial proposal to ultimate completion. It is a maturing, evolving document that hardens and deepens as the project moves through technology and engineering development. In keeping with this concept, the initial plan serves as the mission need statement and is a brief and succinct document.

The plan is tailored to the needs of a particular project, and the format and level of detail will vary with the size, complexity, sensitivity, and other particular characteristics of the project. Generally, the elements of a mature ESAPP are as follows.

Mission Need and Project Objectives   The plan provides a summary of the performance capability to be achieved and outlines technical, resource, and schedule projections. It describes the relationship of the system acquisition project to other research and development efforts and to major thrusts of the National Energy Plan.

Technical Plan   The plan describes the specific scientific, technological, and engineering approaches to meeting performance criteria. Early versions of the technical plan emphasized alternative design approaches to meeting a mission need. As the project matures, the technical plan identifies subsystems and, subsequently, test and verification procedures. In all cases, key technical decision points are identified, to permit optimum designation of approving officials. A specific work breakdown structure is mandatory for each Energy System Acquisition Project.

Risk Assessment   The plan covers project risk assessment and identification of the critical system, subsystem, and other areas that require focused work and resolution. Each risk area identified has a specific plan for overcoming the problem or potential issue in a timely fashion. The impacts of all risks are identified and technical options provided in the assessment. The plan also includes risk assessment of schedule and estimated cost.

Management Approach   The plan covers the organizational responsibilities, decision delegations, and other management arrangements under which the project is to be carried out. It includes identification of key players, supporting organizations, project charters, and other project execution documentation. This section also includes a description of the project management control systems, reporting procedures, and data systems that are used to monitor project status and progress.

Procurement Strategy   The plan describes the approach for processing major items of support described in the Technical Plan Section. As appropriate, this section includes methods of obtaining and sustaining competition, guidelines for acceptance or rejection of projects, decisions about when to solicit, content of solicitations, selection of the type of contract best suited for each stage in the acquisition process, need for developing contractor incentives, and administration of contracts.

Project Schedule   The plan identifies the major milestones up to project completion, includes major procurement actions, and clearly indicates the system acquisition phases and the appropriate decision points.

Resources Plan   The plan includes a total project cost estimate presented by year for all project elements. In-house civil service manpower estimates are presented by installation for the life of the project.

Controlled Items   The plan identifies specific technical, cost, schedule, or other performance parameters for control by the official approving the plan. For these controlled items there is regular reporting and early indication of potential breaching of thresholds agreements.

Annexes   The plan includes two mandatory annexes: Annex One, Environmental Issues and Control Technology, identifies the environmental barriers or questions associated with the specific technology or process and describes the control technology, supporting research, and other program efforts aimed at overcoming environmental constraints or problems. Annex Two, Commercialization and Market Development, develops an early commercialization strategy and matures gradually into a well-defined and comprehensive market development plan.

In keeping with the concept of an evolving, maturing document, the initial ESAPP served as the mission need statement. It was a succinct document (approximately five pages) covering the following points.

Identification of the energy system need in terms of projected market penetration: time of entry, quad requirements, relationship to energy supplies displaced or substituted for, regional characteristics, and general applications.

Assessment of the current state of technology and the potential for existing or known energy systems to meet the identified need, including the results of state-of-the-art assessments: the objective was to ensure that DOE officials have a clear understanding where a specific energy-related technology (for example, direct burning of green wood) stood before initiating any new activity aimed at bringing the particular technology to commercialization. The state-of-the-art assessments covered such elements as the following.

- Status of the technology in terms of current and future market economics

- Cost reduction goals required to meet market characteristics under varying economic assumptions (to include achievements to date and future projections)

- Government involvement and impact to date and future government involvement, if any, and impact

- Gaps in the technology (for example, specific components are not reliable in an operating environment)

- Environmental problems (for example, the current problem of burning green wood and the acceptable level of particulates in stack emissions)

- Current incentives in use and their impact

- Perception of additional incentives and their impact

- Remaining significant political and sociological barriers, e.g., aggregating wood supplies among many small woodlot owners to provide regional supplies within a given area, to support a given size of investment in wood-burning energy-generating facilities

Evaluation of the impact of not meeting the mission need in terms of energy supply shortfalls, economic consequences, environmental concerns, and other institutional or regional effects.

Proposed organizational approach to exploration of alternative design concepts including summary estimates of resource needs, milestone dates, use of governmental and other institutions, management issues, and other questions bearing upon successful execution of the technology development (Phase One).

ENERGY SYSTEM ACQUISITION ADVISORY BOARD

The Energy System Acquisition Advisory Board served as an advisory body to the Secretary on major Energy System Acquisition Projects.

The Board was chaired by the Under Secretary, and it met at his call to review and recommend whether to undertake proposed new major projects or cancel a Project Plan. Reviews by the Board were intended to afford open discussions of issues and alternatives, based upon the most complete presentation of information available, and to ensure that the advice given was as complete and objective as possible. The purpose of the board meetings was to hear all comments in one forum and assist the Under Secretary in arriving at a decision.

The principal members of the Board were the Under Secretary, as chairman, two Deputy Under Secretaries, the Assistant Secretary for Energy Technology, the Acting Assistant Secretary for Conservation and Solar Applications, the Assistant Secretary for Resource Applications, the Acting Assistant Secretary for Environment, the Acting Assistant Secretary for Defense Programs, the Director of the Office of Energy Research, a General Counsel, the Assistant Secretary for Policy and Evaluation, the Controller, and the Director of Procurement and Contracts Management.

Other Assistant Secretaries and program officials were invited to attend as advisors when appropriate. The Assistant Secretary or Director whose major Energy Systems Acquisition Project was presented for decision acted as Assistant Chairman. For decisions on proceeding to commercialization (Key Decision Four) the Assistant Secretary for Resource Applications and/or the Assistant Secretary for Conservation and Solar Applications acted as Assistant Chairman. The Office of the Controller provided staff support to the Chairman of the Advisory Board.

Typically, the documentation for the board meetings was as follows.

- Updated Energy Systems Acquisition Project Plan

- Detailed status and results of work completed

- Specific plans for work to be authorized in ensuing phase

- Cost–benefit analysis

- Updated resource and schedule projections

- Risk assessment, economic analyses, and other supporting data, as necessary

- Impact statements of discontinuing the system

- Comments by each reviewing official

- Independent assessments and evaluation required by previous phase approval.

APPENDIX **E**

ENVIRONMENTAL DEVELOPMENT PLANS AND ENVIRONMENTAL READINESS DOCUMENTS*

Below is a list of the acronyms used in Table E-1, and their proper names.

---

*Peter W. House and Dario R. Monti, *Using Futures Forecasting in the Planning Process,* U.S. Department of Energy, Office of Technology Assessments, Office of the Assistant Secretary for Environment, April 1979.

Table E–1
Examples of the Use of Environmental Development Plans (EDP) and Environmental Readiness Documents (ERD)*

User	How used	Reference
DOE/EV		
MERDI Discussions with local newspaper on MHD facility health issues	1. MERDI Director Jerry Plunkett cited the health concerns identified in the MHD EDP as evidence of DOE's awareness of potential environmental problems of the CDIF. In a letter to Dr. George Rotariu, MERDI staff member Dan Dokan noted that the concerns cited by the paper followed very closely the concerns cited in the EDP. He went on to say, "It is to our advantage to have a document like this to point out to concerned citizens that technical research and development as well as assessments are taking place within this developing technology."	MHD EDP cited in newspaper interview on subject (September 24, 28, 1979).
OES	2. The EDP's and ERD's are being used as input to an overall planning exercise by OES to chart the overall DOE procurement and RD&D cycle with emphasis on where environmental, health, and safety information is factored into decision-making (e.g., procurement requirements, transition points in technology progress (example: pilot to demonstration), and when major federal action affecting the environment is planned (NEPA documents)). This planning exercise will input to the EDP process by recommending improvements.	Conversation with C. Caves, OES, on May 17, 1979.
Office of Program Coordination, Federal Interagency Committee on Health and Environmental Effects of Energy Technologies	3. The EDP's and ERD's are used as planning documents to provide perspective and guidance on the concerns, and thus to define the R&D needs for environmental information and data to the workshop's members. The Oil Shale, Coal Conversion (Liquefaction and Gasification), Fossil Fuel Utilization, MHD, Coal Extraction, and Oil and Gas EDP's were provided to all members prior to the meetings. The workshops aid the coordination of federal environmental R&D.	Workshop on Health and Environmental Effects of Oil Shale, April 1978. Workshop on Health and Environmental Effects on Coal Conversion, August 1979.

DOE/EV/Office of Program Coordination, Office of Health and Environmental Research, and Office of Environmental Compliance and Overview	4. In the preparation of the FY 1981 budget, EDP's and ERD's were used to define environmental, health, and safety concerns and priorities of the energy technologies. These issues are compiled into an annual EV baseline environmental program plan. These plans are used as guidance to EV program staff in selecting task proposals for EV field organizations.	Scheduled Meetings: Workshops for: Coal Extraction Benefication Combustion, June 1979. Oil and Gas (no firm date). ASEV Program Guidance for FY 1981 budget cycle.
DOE/EV/Office of Program Coordination	5. For the annual EV Programmatic Guidance to DOE and its National Laboratories, EDP's and ERD's are used as source documents. The EDP and ERD information is used to guide the preparation of the Laboratory task proposals to be more responsive to the energy technologies environmental, health, and safety issues. The issues in the Programmatic Guidance were derived from the EDP's and ERD's.	ASEV Programmatic Guidance to Field Organizations, February 9, 1979. The EDP is cited among other environmental documents in paragraph 1.c (Basis for Guidance) in the official DOE Programmatic Guidance that is sent to all DOE organizations as part of the formal DOE Call To The Field executed annually by the Comptroller pursuant to the DOE PPBS.
OTI/TAD	6. EDPs provide the basis for generating Annex 1, Project Environmental Plan, to the Energy System Acquisition Project Plans, the baseline documents for DOE's project activities. Information supplied by the EDP's are the environmental concerns and R&D requirements at a programmatic level.	Under Secretary Dale Myer's Interim Policy and Guidance correspondence entitled "Program and Project Management System for DOE Outlay Programs," May 31, 1978.

Table E–1 *continued*

User	How used	Reference
DOE Conservation Program and Health and Environmental Research Program	7. The Conservation Technology Program initiated the following environmental R&D projects as a direct result of the EDP process. • Initial Programmatic EA/EIS on the Electric Car (D. Maxfield, Electric Car Program - Conservation) • Research started on Health Effects of Solar and Heat Engine Working Fluids (M. Minthorn, OHER) • Extensive expansion of Health Effects R&D on Biological Effects from High Voltage Electric Fields (R. Flagna, Electric Energy Systems, ET and M. Minthorn, OHER) • Initiate environmental research characterization study at Pompono Beach on Bioconversion Process (R. Butenhoff, OHER). • Research started at ANL on Health and Environmental Effects of Advance Batteries and Electro Chemical Materials (M. Minthorn, OHER).	Conservation EDP Transportation EDP Electric Energy EDP Energy Storage EDP Buildings and Community Systems, EDP
OHER	8. Nuclear EDP's are used to define the nuclear technology environmental program goals, objectives, and needs for OHER-funded research.	"Environmental Program Needs: Nuclear Technology," W.M. Lowder, April 6, 1979.
OHER	9. The Magnetic Fusion EDP is being used to initiate or redirect research dealing with tritium and magnetic field effects.	Conversations between N. Thomasson and OHER personnel during March 1979.
OHER	10. The Uranium Enrichment EDP is being used to initiate or redirect research dealing with the behavior of uranium hexafluoride in the environment.	Conversations between N. Thomasson and OHER personnel during January–April 1979.

OHER	11. The EDP's were used by the Office of Health and Environmental Research to forecast the technology base/research needs for FY 1981 and beyond for DOE's Assessment Team, R&D Coordination Council. The concerns and research requirements were taken from the EDP's. Thus, the EDP served as a reference source in forecasting technology programs environment R&D needs.	DOE Memorandum; Deutch to Undersecretaries, March 5, 1979.
N(AISP)	12. The Advanced Isotope Separation EDP has stimulated studies on proliferation and is being used to initiate or redirect contractor research dealing with safety and the characterization of particular chemical processes.	Conversations between N. Thomasson and A. Littman and N. Haberman during January–April 1979.
DOE/Technologies **ET/FFE**	1. The Oil Shale EDP was one of the basic documents used by ET/FFE to write the oil shale program management plan submitted to OHB in April, 1979.	ET/FFE, "Oil Shale RD&D Program Management Plan," April 1979.
ET/FFE	2. The planning document states that BETC (the authority organization) is "responsible for managing and coordinating all environmental compliance functions for all EOR and EGR projects, in respect to both ongoing and future projects. "It further stated that this Project Plan Document (PPD) is intended to enable smooth and coordinated implementation of the EOR Environmental Compliance Project and that the PPD has been developed on the basis of the EOR EDP and draft "TIP."	EOR EDP cited as basis for definition of concerns and requirements.
DOE/ET/N	3. This example is one of the major items that EDP's identify . . . the long-range format of DOE-required NEPA actions and documents. Technology offices (even though NEPA guidelines exist) are informed and guided by the EDP Process in forecasting NEPA-required documents. Close coordination with DOE, NEPA, and OGC offices are used in this activity.	AIS EDP

Table E–1 *continued*

User	How used	Reference
OES	During preparation of the joint technology-environmental R&D milestone section of the AIS EDP, it was recognized by the AIS program office that a forecast of the NEPA documents (EA's and EIS's) schedule with long lead start times was necessary to comply with the NEPA law and DOE NEPA regulations. Through TAD's coordination of the AIS office with the OGC and NEPA offices, considerable time and effort was saved by properly scheduling the required lead-time for NEPA documentation milestones with the technology major points.	
ET/N (AISP)	4. The Space Application EDP stimulated early consideration of NEPA requirements, e.g., the EDP identified the need for a programmatic ETS which had not been previously considered.	Conversations between N. Thomasson and ANSP personnel, January–April 1979.
ET/N et. al.	5. The EDPs have fostered enhanced relationships between technology personnel and EV. As an example, Owen Lewis of the ET/N Office of Inertial Confinement has actively sought EV (TAD) assistance in matters pertaining to laser fusions. Such actions have helped establish the role of EV in the overall DOE decision-making process.	Conversation between N. Thomasson and Owen Lewis during preparation of the Project Environmental Plan for the NOVA project, April 1979.
RA (URE)	6. The Uranium Enrichment EDP identified the need for new or modified research dealing with affluent controls and environmental behavior analysis.	Conversation between N. Thomasson and URE personnel during preparation of Project Environmental Plans, April 1979.

DOE/General John O'Leary, Deputy Secretary, DOE	1. The Coal/Oil Mixtures ERD was the basic planning document used by Coal/Oil Mixtures Task Force headed by J. O'Leary, April 1979.	William Wilson, EV/OTI/TAD, Coal/Oil Mixtures ERD, April 12, 1979 (transmittal date).
ET/M and EV/OHER	2. The Magnetic Fusion EDP identified areas in which inter-program research can be used to the mutual benefit of more than one DOE organization, e.g., the OHER electric and magnetic field work in support of electric transmission and magnetohydrodynamics will be of value to similar ET/M work underway in support of magnetic fusion, and vice versa.	Discussions during March 1979 meeting of the Environmental Coordinating Committee Subcommittee on Magnetic Fusion.
ET and EV	3. EDP's and ERD's are used by both offices (e.g., FFE, Solar, Geothermal OHER) as the basic planning documents for the environmental sections for their multiyear program plans. In some cases, the EDP is used as the individual environmental program plan.	Ron Losse, ET/S Charles Edington, OHER James Swinebroad, OHER
ORNL, Environmental and Health Program Plan, Pike County Coal Gasification Facility	4. Under the definition of issues and requirements, the plan cites the Coal Gasification EDP as the basis for a number of environmental and health concerns discussed in the plan. In describing the scope of the EDP, the plan says "It identifies environmental issues, requirements, and projects related to both high and low-Btu gasification and considers the energy technology from the preparation of coal to the end use of the gas."	Gasification EDP cited in plan.
Other Organizations OTA/CEQ	1. Other governmental agencies conducting energy technology assessments and various environmental activities, as well as the private sector, use EDP's as information sources: • The Office of Technology Assessment, U.S. Congress requested the Biomass EDP for use in conducting one of their technology assessments of solar energy; • The Council on Environmental Quality (CEQ) has also requested EDPs for use in its work; and	

Table E–1 *continued*

User	How used	Reference
	• Brookhaven National Laboratory (BNL) as well as other national laboratories have requested solar EDPs as reference and information sources.	
Nuclear Regulatory Commission	2. The Uranium Mining, Milling, and Conversion EDP is being used as a tool for identifying the work of other agencies that is relevant to NRC responsibilities, and is being used by NRC as a mechanism for interagency contacts and coordination.	Letter from W. Dircks, NRC, to Dario Monti, DOE, December 1, 1978.
Nuclear Regulatory Commission	3. The Uranium Mining, Milling, and Conversion EDP is being used to prepare a position paper on NRC responsibilities for uranium mining.	Conversation between R. Grill, NRC, and N. Thomasson, DOE, April 16, 1979.
DOE/EPA/HEW	4. Under a Memorandum of Understanding (MOU) executed among HEW, EPA, and DOE in response to the President's March 1977 energy message, which directed these three agencies to coordinate their activities relative to programs involving emerging energy technologies, EDP's serve as DOE's primary environmental planning documents.	The DOE/EPA/HEW ad hoc group has held two meetings relative to the March 1977 presidential directive to date. In these meetings, DOE used the Oil Shale and Coal Gasification and Liquefaction EDP's as examples of the agency's environmental planning for emerging energy technologies.
DOE/EPA	5. DOE used the EDP as the basic source of information in their coordination with EPA on the NEPA compliance and associated supportive R&D responsibilities required for emerging energy technologies.	In the MOU that exists between DOE and EPA (exclusive of the DOE/EPA/HEW) on NEPA compliance and associated supportive R&D, the EDP is specified as the formal

Organization of Economic Corporation and Development, OECD Conference	6. Dr. Comar of EPRI cited and discussed the Coal Gasification and Liquefaction EDPs are examples of good overall environmental plans for particular technologies. They were also cited in the discussion of how site-specific problems can be identified and addressed in the context of an overall plan.	agency document for apprising EPA of DOE's formal plans for addressing these issues. EDPs cited in presentation as example of complete environmental plan.
ORNL, Environmental and Health Program Plan, University of Minnesota, Gasifier Facility	7. The Gasification EDP was cited in the plan as the basis for the issues and requirements discussed in the plan. It stated "this particular Environmental Development Plan is intended to be the basic DOE document for environmental R&D planning, management, and review related to DOE's Coal Gasification Program . . . "We have used them (issues and requirements) as guides to ensure consideration of the complete range of environmental activities in developing our proposed monitoring and testing program."	Gasification EDP cited plan.
Public Various environmental and conservation organizations representing public environmental interests	1. DOL's Commercialization Task Force Reports, accompanied by the 16 EDR's, were released to the public for comment. DOE was commended collectively by environmental and conservation organizations for the high quality of the environmental assessment of the technology options performed by the Office of Environment. The ERD's served DOE well in communicating to the public the Department's commitment to a cost-effective, environmentally compatible energy strategy.	Letter to Dr. James R. Schlesinger and Jackson Gonraud, DOE, from Environmental Groups (Environmental Action, Friends of the Earth, Natural Resources Defense Council, Sierra Club, Solar Lobby and the Environmental Policy Center) dated November 14, 1978.
Weekly Reader	2. The Weekly Reader is a "paper" distributed to elementary school children throughout the U.S.A. The	William Wilson, EV/OTI/TAD, transmittal letter to

Table E–1 *continued*

User	How used	Reference
	Coal Extraction and Preparation, Coal Liquefaction, Coal Gasification, and Direct Combustion EDP's were used to delineate the environmental concerns associated with coal usage for this paper.	Miss Isabelle Abrams, c/o Weekly Reader, dated December 18, 1978.
Distribution to Foreign Nations (UK, Germany, Sweden, France, others)	3. At international meeting, the EDP's and ERD's are given to representatives of foreign nations as examples of DOE's environmental planning and assessments process. At the Energy Technology Workshop at Paris in February 1979, selected EDP's and ERD's were provided to Great Britain, Norway, and Sweden by EV/OPC. At the April 1979 meeting at DOE, Lord Flowers, Head of the United Kingdom's Committee on Energy and Environment, complemented EV for this class of documents. A full set of EDP's and ERD's are being provided to his committee. At other foreign meetings, selected EDP's have been provided to representatives from Belgium, Germany, and Nairobe.	DOE letter to D. Monti, TAD from G. Shepherd, OPC May 1979.

*Peter W. House and Dario R. Monti, *Using Future Forecasting in the Plan Process*, Appendix D.

AIS   Advanced Isotope Separation
AISP   Advanced Isotope Separation Program
ANL   Argonne National Lab
ANSP   Advanced Nuclear Systems Program
ASEV   Assistant Secretary for Environment, DOE
BETC   Bartlesville Energy Technology Center
BNL   Brookhaven National Laboratory
CDIF   Component development and integration facility
CEQ   Council on Environmental Quality
COE   Corps of Engineers, U.S. Army
DOE   Department of Energy
EA   Environmental Assessment
EGR   Enhanced Gas Recovery
EIS   Environmental Impact Statement

EOR Enhanced Oil Recovery
EPRI Electric Power Research Institute
EPA Environmental Protection Agency
ET Office of Energy Technology, DOE
EV Office of Environment, DOE
FFE Office of Fossil Fuel Energy, ET
FFEE Office of Fossil Fuels Energy Environmental Controls, ET
HEW Health, Education and Welfare
MERDI Montana Energy Research and Development Institute
MHD magnetohydrodynamic
MOU Memorandum of Understanding
N (in ET/N) Office of Nuclear Technology, ET
N(AISP) Office of Nuclear Technology, Advanced Isotopic Space Power
NEPA National Environmental Policy Act
NOVA Neodymium Glass Laser (named for astronomical "nova")
NRC Nuclear Regulatory Commission
OES Office of Environment and Safety, DOE
OECD, Organization of Economic Co-Operation and Development
OGC Office of General Counsel, DOE
OHER Office of Health and Environmental Research, EV, DOE
OPC Office of Program Coordination
OTA Office of Technology Assessments
OTI Office of Technology Impacts, EV, DOE
PPBS Planning, Programming and Budgeting System
PPD Project Plan Document
RA Resource Applications (Office of)
R&D Research and Development
RD&D research, development, and demonstration
S (in ET/S) Office of Solar Technology, ET
TAD Technology Assessments Division, 071, EV, DOE
TIP Technology Implementation Plan
URE Uranium Enrichment Program

APPENDIX **F**

PRIORITIZATION OF ENVIRONMENTAL ISSUES*

TECHNOLOGIES AND ISSUES

The first step in developing a scoring technique is to select appropriate sets of technologies and environmental issues. Each technology should represent a discrete method of energy production or utilization. Each issue should represent a discrete causative factor that can result in an environmental, health, or safety impact. Further, the number of technologies and issues selected should be manageable. Figure F-1 depicts the elements of the scoring technique for each issue and technology.

The national energy goals require involvement in five resource areas: solar, geothermal, fossil, nuclear, and conservation. Conservation is considered a resource in the sense that it makes energy available from hitherto wasted or inefficiently used resources. The specific technologies addressed in each of the resource areas are listed in Table F-1.

The environmental issues selected for ranking are listed in Table F-2. They represent a set of 59 causative factors that can result in health, safety, ecology, or socioeconomic impacts. Statements generally defining the issues and linking them to probable environmental

*Department of Energy, Office of the Assistant Secretary for Environment, *Strategic Plan,* Draft (March 1980), pp. 30–42.

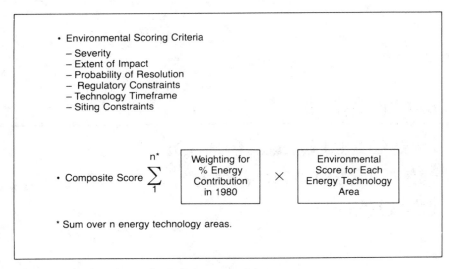

Figure F-1. Scoring of environmental issues.

impacts were developed from information in the EDP's, PEP's, and the Annual Environmental Analysis Report.

Issue Ranking

No ranking scheme can be absolute. The "importance" of an issue can be gauged from the seriousness of the environmental problems for one or more technologies, or it can be deduced from the fact that the issue surfaces for a large number of technologies that, in the aggregate, represent a large fraction of the Nation's total energy resources. The ranking system used for this analysis resulted in specifying a Composite Environmental Score for each issue by:

- Identifying the environmentally serious issues for each technology
- Assigning environmental scores to the issues
- Weighting for energy contributions

The environmental scores for each technology took into account the degree of severity, the extent of the impact (the possibility of long-term or short-term exposure, population affected, and expected number of exposures), the probability of resolution within a foreseeable time frame, the ability to meet existing environmental regulations, the technology time frame, and the siting constraints.

Table F–1
Energy Technologies

Nuclear
- Uranium mining
- Uranium milling
- Uranium conversion
- Uranium enrichment
- Light-water reactor
- Nuclear materials transportation
- Decontamination and decommissioning
- Advanced isotope separation
- Magnetic fusion
- Liquid-metal fast-breeder reactor
- Space applications
- Away from reactor storage
- High-level waste storage
- Reprocessing
- Special nuclear materials (weapons)

Fossil
- Coal production
- Coal utility and industrial boilers
- Oil extraction
- Oil refining and storage
- Oil-fired utility and industrial boilers
- Oil, transportation end use
- Gas production
- Gas-fired utility and industrial boilers
- Coal gasification
- Coal liquefaction
- Oil shale
- Enhanced oil recovery
- Magnetohydrodynamics
- Fossil-fuel utilization

Solar
- Solar heating and cooling of buildings
- Solar agricultural and industrial process heat
- Solar thermal power systems
- Biomass
- Alcohol fuels
- Wind energy systems
- Photovoltaics
- Ocean thermal energy conversion
- Solar power satellite
- Geothermal

Conservation
- Transportation heat engines
- Electric and hybrid vehicles
- Light-duty diesel
- Electric energy systems
- Battery storage
- Nonbattery storage
- Building and community systems
- Urban waste
- Industrial programs

Issues pertinent to technologies expected to reach commercialization during 1987 to 1995 received additional emphasis, because expenditures during 1982 to 1986 were likely to have the most direct effect on technologies commercialized during this period.

The projected national and regional trends (Figure F-2) for several regulated and unregulated pollutants given in the Annual Environmental Analysis Report, along with the analyses of concerns given in the EDP's for the respective technologies, form the bases for the issue scores. The relative energy contributions of the technologies within each resource area were derived from the National Energy Plan. All 59 issues defined in Table F-2 were ranked.

IMPORTANT ISSUES FOR EMERGING
ENERGY TECHNOLOGIES

Although the general scoring method provides a ranking of environmental issues, the method emphasizes the commercial technolo-

Table F–2
Environmental Issues

Specific issue	Issue statement
Airborne active particulates	Health impacts of fine particulates capable of remaining airborne, generally found in association with suspected carcinogenic compounds.
Airborne inert particulates	Fungitive dust from mining, preparation, and process operations that may create visibility impairment and health hazards.
Airborne hydrocarbons	Hydrocarbons released into the atmosphere, and their control.
Airborne organics	Release of organic compounds to the atmosphere or workplace from fugitive, exhaust, and evaporate emissions.
Aerosols	Release of aerosols (e.g., cooling tower drift, oil refineries) during plant operations resulting in transport of chemicals.
Airborne trace and heavy metals	Trace and heavy metals (unregulated/regulated) in airborne emissions (fugitive and point sources).
Carbon monoxide	Emissions of carbon monoxide from increased fossil fuel use, after employment of control technology.
Carbon dioxide	Global accumulation of carbon dioxide in the troposphere due to combustion of fossil fuels.
Oxides of sulfur	Emissions of oxides of sulfur from increased fossil fuel usage that may result in acid rains or other health impacts after employment of control technology.
Other sulfur compounds in air	Emissions of sulfur compounds other than SO_x that are known to be toxic (e.g., H_2S and SF_6).
Oxides of nitrogen	Emissions of oxides of nitrogen due to increasing direct use of coal and production of synthetic fuels, and difficulties of controlling the emissions.
Other nitrogen compounds in air	Emissions of nitrogen compounds other than NO_x (e.g., NH_3) into work or public places.
Airborne halogen compounds	Release of toxic halogen gases in the workplace or to the environment.
Other gaseous emissions	Release of gases from specific processes (e.g., naphtha from fuel cells, arsine from battery-charging into workplace environments.
Airborne radionuclides	Fugitive release of radioactive gases and particles into the atmosphere.
Airborne pathogens/fungi	Bacteria, mold, and fungi buildup due to waste materials, increased humidity, or ventilation changes.
Odors	Noxious odors from process operations.
Ozone/oxidants	Generation of ozone and smog-related chemicals from power plants, transportation sector, and ultra-high-voltage electrical transmission lines.

Table F–2 *continued*

Specific issue	Issue statement
Pesticides and herbicides	Increase use of chemicals and pesticides for biomass production, weed removal.
Other fugitives	Atmospheric release of air pollutants from insulation in buildings, freon from uranium enrichment, SHACOB, and SAIPH processes, and cyanides from biomass conversions.
Total dissolved solids	Discharges of dissolved compounds (e.g., salts) from process operations and power plant cooling, affecting local ecosystems and water supplies.
Total suspended solids	Dirt and silt from mine and waste pile runoff entering surface waters.
Biochemical oxygen demand	Releases of biologically active residuals to water that may use up the available oxygen for life support.
Brines	Brine runoff into surface and groundwaters from mines.
Acids in water	Changes in acidity of surface and groundwater from leachates, acid mine runoff, storage and waste piles.
Alkalines in water	Changes in alkalinity of surface and groundwater from alkaline waste.
Biocides and inhibitors in water	Release of additives and inhibitors into surface waters from heat storage systems, secondary oil recovery operations.
Oil and gases in water	Accidental releases and leaks of petroleum products into water supplies.
Waterborne radionuclides	Release of radioactive materials into the water sources.
Toxic/hazardous compounds in water	Impacts on surface and groundwaters arising from use and disposal of potentially toxic or hazardous working fluids.
Discharge of process residuals in water	Process residuals from various operations that may be released into surface and underground waters.
Metals and metallic compounds in water	Discharge of trace quantities of metal into water supplies and treatment plants.
Leachates and organics in water	Leachates from waste and storage piles and in situ operations affecting ground and surface waters.
Disposal of noncombustible residuals	Disposal of dry noncumbustible solid wastes after energy extraction (e.g., spent shale) or ashes from plant operations.
Industrial sludges	Disposal of possibly hazardous wet residues from plant operations, and environmental control cleanup sludges (e.g., FGD waste).
Nuclear solid wastes	Accumulation and management of large amounts of radioactive waste tailings from the nuclear fuel cycle.

Table F–2 *continued*

Specific issue	Issue statement
High-level nuclear solid wastes	Storage and management of high-level radioactive wastes over centuries.
Low-level nuclear solid wastes	Management of large amounts of low-level radioactive wastes (e.g., contaminated equipment, expended filters).
Disposal of other solid wastes	Construction and startup wastes (e.g., drilling muds), close-down and abandonment of equipment (e.g., batteries), and special materials (e.g., spent catalysts).
Water use conflicts	Siting constraints due to unavailability of large quantities of process water in arid regions.
Land use conflicts	Siting constraints due to conflict between new and traditional uses of available land.
Conflicting use of scarce materials	Competing use of scarce metals, alloys, and food crops which are traditionally used for nonenergy-producing purposes.
Terrestrial ecosystem disruption	Disruption of natural terrestrial ecosystems by energy facilities during normal operations.
Land surface disruption	Disruption of natural contours of land surfaces through mining or erosion.
Land subsidence	Land subsidence due to mining, water depletion, or drilling operations.
Seismicity enhancement	Inducement of earthquakes by pressure release and fluid removal during resource extraction.
Electric and magnetic	Exposure to high-level electric and magnetic fields (e.g., HVAC, high-strength magnets) and microwaves.
Thermal discharges	Thermal loads to the environment (air, water, or ground) affecting ecosystems and local weather (microclimate).
Noise	Control of noise sources during facility operations.
Building ventilation changes	Indoor air pollution from reduced air ventilation in buildings and homes.
Decontamination and decommissioning	Reclamation of the facilities and land used for nuclear and synfuel operations.
Occupational hazards from facility accidents	Occupational hazards from energy technologies due to facility accidents.
Occupation hazards from fires and explosions	Occupational hazards due to probability of fires and explosions in energy facilities.
Occupational exposure to hazardous materials	Worker contact with toxic and hazardous working fluids or other hazards during normal facility operations.
Occupational radiation exposure	Worker exposure to ionizing radiation from nuclear power plants and laser radiation in AIS plants.
Public hazards from fuel transportation	Public hazards from accidents during the bulk transportation of energy resources (coal, oil, LNG, nuclear fuels).

Table F-2 *continued*

Specific issue	Issue statement
Public hazards from facility accidents	Public hazards from facility malfunction or accidents involving energy facilities.
Public exposure to hazards	Public contact with new and unfamiliar hazards from energy technologies such as electric shock and decreased performance of products.
Socioeconomics	Societal implications of environmental impacts and siting of energy technologies.

gies because of their relatively high energy contributions. The method did not highlight those issues that have special significance for one or more of the emerging technologies.

To identify those issues that would have special importance for a strategy weighted toward the emerging sector, three criteria were applied to the findings of the general method:

- The issue was among the first 25 issues ranked by the general scoring method.

- The environmental parameters without the energy contribution factor, termed the "acuteness factor" for the issue, scored high for one or more technologies in the emerging sector.

- The issue was ranked among the first 25 issues when only emerging technologies were considered.

Only the following nine issues meet all three criteria simultaneously:

- Airborne trace and heavy metals

- Airborne active particles

- Airborne radionuclides

- Disposal of noncombustible residuals

- Water use conflicts

- Sulfur oxides

- Airborne organics

- Leachates and organics in water

- Airborne hydrocarbons

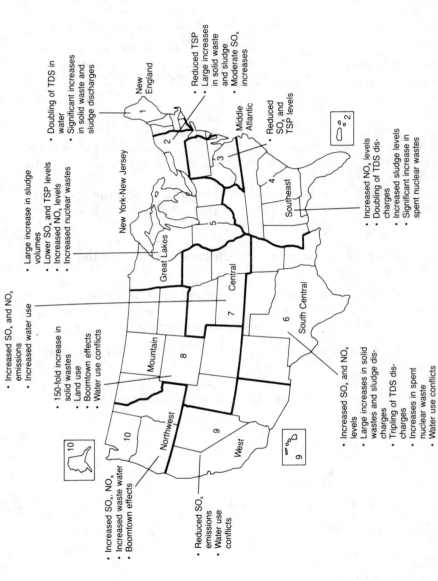

Figure F-2. Regional shifts in environmental pollutant levels between 1975 and 2000. TDS, total dissolved solids (in water); TSP, total suspended particulates (in air).

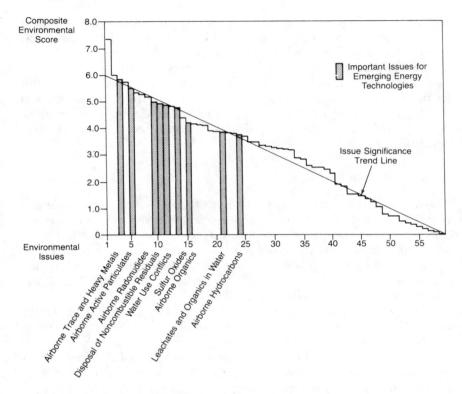

Figure F-3. Relative significance of environmental issues.

Figure F-3 highlights the nine important issues for emerging energy technologies.

Airborne Trace and Heavy Metals

Trace and heavy metals in the air can affect ecosystems and human health. The long-term effects of the accumulation of metals in living organisms are of concern. Lead emissions from motor vehicles are currently the only ones regulated under the Clean Air Act and Amendments.

Metals are released into the atmosphere along with the products of combustion of fossil fuels and urban waste. Trace metals are released in the workplace environment during uranium mining, milling, and conversion operations and during the manufacture of batteries and photovoltaic cells. The EDP's for these programs address the issue. Thus, it is the predominant issues of commercialized technologies (coal, oil, and nuclear) that contribute a significant portion to the Nation's energy needs. The acuteness of the issue has been rated high for oil shale technology.

Information on national emission levels of different trace and heavy metals is incomplete. The transport and fate of these metals in the terrestrial ecosystems are extremely complex problems and need to be assessed along with the related issues of metals and metallic compounds in water, process residuals in water, and other solid waste residuals.

Airborne Active Particulates

Active particulates are small particles of hazardous materials that can remain suspended in air for long periods. Hazardous ingredients are also sometimes found covering hte surface of, or in association with, small inert particles, the combination being potentially hazardous. Of particular concern are the fine particulates (with aerodynamic diameters of under 3 microns), which can penetrate deep lung tissue, where they may be retained.

Active particulates pose several concerns. The fine particulates are difficult to measure and characterize. The number of associated compounds is formidable. For example, diesel vehicle particulate emissions are known to be associated with over 30,000 organic compounds. Included in these compounds are polynuclear aromatics, which are known to have carcinogenic properties. In addition, synergistic effects of the compounds with each other and with carbonaceous or other particulates are not understood at present. Extensive in vitro or in vivo health effect studies are needed.

The acuteness of the issue has been judged high from analyses presented in related documents for oil shale, coal gasification, and coal liquefaction technologies. These technologies are critical to the success of the national policy of reducing oil imports. For light-duty diesel vehicles, small particulates are an extremely critical issue. The EPA's final standards for total fine particulate emissions of light-duty diesel vehicles specify stringent limits for 1981 and 1985. Compliance with the 1985 standard of 0.2 gram per vehicle mile has been considered extremely difficult by several vehicle manufacturers. Similar particulate standards are likely for heavy-duty trucks and stationary diesel power plants.

Active particulates are also associated with all fossil-fuel combustion sources, including magnetohydrodynamics. Power plants of this type may not be commercialized in the United States until 1995 to 2000, but if the known particulate emissions cannot be controlled, further delays may be encountered.

Current utility particulate emissions can be controlled by filtration or electrostatic precipitation. Reduction in particulate emissions from electric utilities and industrial combustion sources will be largely off-set by increases due to fossil-fuel processing, transportation and storage, and use of residential wood burning. About 5 million tons per year are estimated in 2000 without mobile sources or residential wood burning included. Projections indicate that particulate emissions from energy sources will increase significantly in the South Central States owing to a shift to utility coal burning and increased residential wood burning.

Airborne Radionuclides

Radioactive airborne emissions from power reactors (light-water reactors and liquid-metal fast-breeder reactors) give rise to two types of health concern. The first concern is the exposure of the population residing near the reactor site. This concern is small because the local radiation levels in the surrounding area are controlled to low limits that are negligible relative to normal background levels. The second concern is the potential accumulation of long-lived radioisotopes (e.g., krypton-85, carbon-14, iodine-129, and tritium) in the biosphere over a long period of time, which may pose long-term public exposure risks and which may affect the atmospheric ionization layer, causing weather modifications. This issue requires further study because of the uncertainties associated with the health risks of low-level exposure and the effect on the ionization layer. If the studies confirm that there is a long-term problem, control technology will be required on operating plants to reduce the releases of long-lived radioisotopes to an acceptable level. Light-water reactors will contribute approximately 10 quads by 1990.

Radioactive emissions can result from other segments of the nuclear fuel cycle. These include radon gas and its particulate daughters from uranium mines and mills, and uranium isotopes from conversion, enrichment, and fuel fabrication facilities. Spent-fuel storage facilities may release small quantities of krypton-85 and iodine-131 or iodine-129 if defective fuel is stored. When spent fuel is recycled or reprocessed, reprocessing plants and vitrification facilities could release small amounts of krypton-85, iodine-129, tritium, and carbon-14 as well as some transuranics. Radon releases from uranium mill tailings and the long-term control of the tailings will be limited by Nuclear Regulatory Commission regulations and provisions of the Uranium Mill Tailings Radiation Control Act of 1978. In addition, the Environmental Protection Agency has declared radionuclides hazardous air emissions and is now in the process of establishing stringent standards for the control of all radioactive, man-made emissions. These new requirements will have to be studied to determine the impact on existing and emerging technologies.

Disposal of Noncombustible Residuals

The issue of the disposal of noncombustible solid wastes generated at energy-producing facilities concerns their safe disposal and long-term isolation from the environment. Sources of these wastes include coal-fired boiler ash, spent shale after shale oil retorting, and coal gasification and liquefaction of solid residuals. These technologies will contribute approximately 32 quads by 1990. The wastes may contain toxic or trace elements that could enter into ground and surface waters if not properly controlled. Future regulations under the Resource Conservation and Recovery Act will be used to manage these wastes effectively. Minimal data are available on the wastes from the newer technologies, and the impact of regulations is uncertain. The issue is thus tied to leachates and organics in water and toxic and hazardous fluids in water.

It is projected that, nationally, the noncombustible solid wastes will increase from 52 million tons per year in 1975 to 714 million tons per year in 2000, a 1300-percent increase. The heaviest impacts will be felt in the oil-shale-producing regions of the Mountain States. Inadequate measures for dealing with the problem could lead to significant environmental risk in Colorado and Utah, especially in terms of water quality impacts in a water-scarce region and on potential reclamation of spoil sites. The South South Central States may also become a major contributor of noncombustible solid waste and sludges by the year 200, due to increased coal combustion.

Water Use Conflicts

A fourfold increase in water consumption by the Nation's energy industry is expected between 1975 and 2000. Growth in steam electric generation by coal and nuclear-fueled facilities would place added burdens on already limited supplies in many areas. Water shortages and conflicts with traditional agricultural and other industrial roles may be a primary barrier to siting energy facilities in the South Central, Central, Mountain, and Northwestern States.

The conflicting use of scarce water supplies is also a major issue in coal and uranium mining and oil shale processing, which will contribute approximately 55 percent of the energy demand by 1990. These technologies must be sited near available water resources.

Coal mining and revegetation of stripped mines is water-intensive and is a major concern in the Western States, where the majority of strip-mining occurs. These surface mines will be competing with area agricultural users for available water. The Surface Mining Control and Reclamation Act of 1976 regulates the use of groundwater, but its full application in a number of settings has not been fully demonstrated. Uranium mine dewatering also results in the depletion of larger quantities of groundwater that cannot be reused.

Of the emerging technologies, the production of oil from oil-shale surface retorting is the most water-intensive. Up to 3 barrels of water for every barrel of shale oil produced are estimated to be required for the operation of the retorts and compaction of the spent-shale wastes. Methods of recycling and conserving water require further development.

Sulfur Oxides

Sulfur oxides are by-products of fossil-fuel combustion that can be transported long distances in the air. They react with airborne water, resulting in acid rains over widespread regions. The acid rain increases the acidity of surface waters, which results in the mortality of many species of fish in the Northeastern and North Central United States.

Sulfur oxides emissions from new power plants and 26 other industrial categories are regulated by the New Source Performance Standards under the Clean Air Act, as amended. Emissions from existing sources are required to be reduced in accordance with the applicable State Implementation Plans. Energy sources were responsible for releasing approximately 26 million tons of sulfur oxides in 1975 and are expected to reduce their contribution to about 25 million tons per year in 2000 with the employment of the Best Available Control Technology. Even so, the quantities will remain very significant. Secondary issues of environmental control process sludge disposal (industrial sludges) will also assume importance. Sulfur oxides levels will increase in the South Central States, which are expected to produce almost half of the Nation's sulfur and nitrogen oxides emissions by the year 2000.

For enhanced oil recovery, sulfur oxides emissions are an acute problem in California because of that state's stringent emission standards. The emissions are released by the auxiliary power generation equipment.

Airborne Organics

Releases of organic compounds to the atmosphere or workplace from fugitive, exhaust, and evaporative emissions are potential hazards to public and occupational health. Technologies that release organics include oil refining, uranium enrichment, coal gasification and liquefaction, and diesel engines. High acuteness factors have been judged for the coal gasification and liquefaction technologies.

One class of organic compounds, the hydrocarbons, is regulated under the Clean Air Act (as amended) and is treated as a separate issue.

Organic compounds of concern in this issue are a class of high-molecular-weight compounds known as polycyclic organic matter. Organic compounds are generally associated with fine and coarse particulates found in fossil-fuel combustion exhaust products. Polycyclic organic matter contains a number of compounds potentially hazardous to human health, and information on its biological activity in the human respiratory tract is limited.

The production of synthetic liquid and gaseous fuels from coal results in fugitive emissions of dangerous hydrogen cyanide and sulfur-containing heterocyclic organic compounds. The main concern in this case is occupational health and safety.

Evaporative emissions of trichloroethylene occur in uranium enrichment plants. Other organic liquids are used as working fluids for solar agricultural and industrial process heat and solar heating and cooling of buildings.

Organics are present also in the exhaust products of urban-waste combusion and cocumbustion facilities.

Leachates and Organics in Water

The issue arises from the possibility of surface water and groundwater contamination by leachates from the large quantities of solid wastes and sludges that are characteristic of coal, oil extraction, and oil shale technologies. Leaching of rain runoff water from abandoned coal mines and underground coal gasification or oil-shale in-situ retorting operations is also of concern. Controls are feasible in all cases but may be difficult to implement correctly because of their high costs.

Uncertainties about local leachate containment requirements and the hazardous waste provisions of the Resource Conservation and Recovery Act dictate that the environmental impacts of mining and in-situ operations be carefully assessed prior to the decision for proceeding with each major demonstration or plant construction.

The issue has been judged to have a high acuteness factor for oil shale and coal liquefaction technologies because of the potentially hazardous compounds present in the waste from these technologies. Biomass conversion wastes and urban-waste noncombustible portions, after separation from the combustible refuse-derived fuel portion, contain large quantities of organics that may also contaminate water supplies. Research requirements for this issue should be evaluated in conjunction with the related issues of noncombustible residuals and industrial sludges.

Airborne Hydrocarbons

Atmospheric release of non-methane hydrocarbons from stationary sources, electric utilities, and petroleum refineries will increase some 23 percent over 1975 levels by the year 2000, even if fully controlled to meet Point Source Emission Standards. During this same period mobile-source emissions will decrease substantially throughout the Nation due to more stringent controls. Because the stationary sources account for only about 20 percent of the total hydrocarbon emissions, levels are projected to decrease overall.

A very large number of technologies are responsible for hydrocarbon emissions. The acuteness factor for the issue has been judged high for coal liquefaction technology, where hydrocarbons may occur as fugitive emissions. For light-duty diesel vehicles, if exhaust gas recirculation is used to control nitrogen oxides emissions, an increase in hydrocarbon, carbon monoxide, and particulate emissions is likely to result.

OTHER IMPORTANT ISSUES

Some important issues may appear to have been overlooked in the eight issues discussed so far. The procedure used in the selection of these issues emphasized technologies that will emerge in the 1987 to 1995 time frame and technologies that are likely to meet severe siting constraints due to local-regulations or collocation with other technologies with severe environmental impacts. Notably, oil shale, high-level nuclear waste storage, coal gasification, and coal liquefaction are in this group. The ranking procedure recognizes the large energy contribution of existing technologies using oil, natural gas, and nuclear resources, amounting to 90 percent of the energy needs in 1990. The first ten issues pertain to all commercialized technologies using these resources.

The selection of important issues for these technologies has to be made on the basis of the cumulative effects of their continued or increased use, rather than the severity or "acuteness" of their local impacts. Three issues of particular importance to fossil-fuel combustion are carbon dioxide, sulfur oxides, and nitrogen oxides. Carbon dioxide accumulation is of concern because of the "greenhouse effect" of its accumulation, and the gaseous oxides of sulfur and nitrogen are the major man-made precursors of the formation of acid rains.

Continuing accumulation of carbon dioxide in the troposphere can effect serious climatic changes throughout the world and possibly cause flooding of coastal lands from the melting of polar ice cap fringes. Increased coal combustion will result in increasing annual carbon dioxide emissions in the United States by almost 20 percent (over 1975 levels) by the year 2000, to some 3300 million tons per year. Many important questions relating to the transport, fate, and effects of carbon dioxide accumulation need to be answered, and a better understanding of global emissions, both man-made and natural, is needed.

The main contributor to acid rains is believed to be emissions of sulfur oxides from coal-burning power plants. The transport and fate of sulfur dioxide emissions from coal combustion have been under intensive study. Emissions from new power plants are regulated under the strict New Source Performance Standards. Emissions from plants built before 1971 are, of course, less stringently controlled. Although nationwide emission levels may decline somewhat by 2000, local increases are expected in the South Central Region.

Oxides of nitrogen are also suspected to contribute to acid rains by the formation of nitrates in the atmosphere. These emissions will increase in 2000 by 32 percent over 1975 levels, even though their major nonenergy source, the transportation sector, is likely to reduce its emission levels to meet stricter standards. Two approaches have been taken to control nitrogen oxides emissions from utility contribution: combustion modifications and scrubbing. Combustion modification is effective in reducing emissions by 20 to 60 percent. Further reductions would require scrubbing, which is reported to have been successfully demonstrated in Japan.

Index